AF352201

Criminal Justice
Recent Scholarship

Edited by
Marilyn McShane and Frank P. Williams III

A Series from LFB Scholarly

Drug Use and Delinquency
Causes of Dropping Out of High School?

Joseph M. Gasper

LFB Scholarly Publishing LLC
El Paso 2012

Copyright © 2012 by LFB Scholarly Publishing LLC

All rights reserved.

Library of Congress Cataloging-in-Publication Data

Gasper, Joseph M., 1980-
  Drug use and delinquency : causes of dropping out of high school? /
Joseph M. Gasper.
     p. cm. -- (Criminal justice: recent scholarship)
  Includes bibliographical references and index.
  ISBN 978-1-59332-491-9 (hbk. : alk. paper)
  1. High school dropouts--Social conditions--United States. 2. High
school dropouts--Drug use--United States. 3. Problem youth--Drug
use--United States. 4. Juvenile delinquency--United States. I. Title.
  LC146.6.G37 2012
  373.12'9130973--dc23
                                        2011036656

ISBN 978-1-59332-491-9

Printed on acid-free 250-year-life paper.

Manufactured in the United States of America.

Table of Contents

List of Tables vii

List of Figures...xi

Acknowledgements...xiii

Chapter 1: Drug Use, Delinquency, and Dropout 1

Chapter 2: Causes of Dropout..7

Chapter 3: Distinguishing Causes from Symptoms 29

Chapter 4: Explaining Drug Use, Delinquency, and Dropout..............51

Chapter 5: Toward a Theory of Precocious Development 79

Endnotes 99

Appendix...105

References...189

Index 203

List of Tables

Table A-1. Summary of prior studies on delinquency, drug use, and dropout — 106

Table A- 2. Controls included by prior studies — 113

Table A- 3. Variable definitions — 115

Table A-4. Items used to create delinquency and drug use scales — 121

Table A-5. Restrictions to obtain final NLSY97 sample — 124

Table A-6. Number of person-years observations contributed by youth — 124

Table A- 7. Descriptive statistics, pooled — 125

Table A- 8. Comparison of included and excluded youth in 1997 — 131

Table A- 9. Descriptive statistics for delinquency and drug use — 135

Table A- 10. Comparison of dropouts and non-dropouts in 1997, by poverty status — 137

Table A- 11. Dropout status in 1998 by delinquency in 1997, by poverty status — 142

Table A- 12. Dropout status in 1998 by drug use in 1997, by poverty status — 145

Table A- 13. Regressions of dropout on delinquency — 146

Table A- 14. Regressions of dropout on drug use — 150

Table A- 15. Regressions of dropout on delinquency and drug use — 154

Table A- 16. Summary of regressions of dropout on delinquency, by offense type — 158

Table A- 17. Summary of regressions of dropout on drug use, by drug type — 161

Table A- 18. Summary of alternative model specifications for delinquency — 162

Table A- 19. Summary of alternative model specifications for drug use — 166

Table A- 20. Regressions of dropout on delinquency, interaction with poverty status — 170

Table A- 21. Regressions of dropout on drug use, interaction with poverty status — 171

Table A- 22. Summary of regressions of dropout on delinquency and drug use, interaction with alternative measure of poverty status — 172

Table A- 23. Regressions of dropout on delinquency, interactions with social sanctions — 173

Table A- 24. Regressions of dropout on drug use, interactions with social sanctions — 174

Table A- 25. Regressions of dropout on delinquency, interactions with social sanctions and poverty status — 175

Table A- 26. Regressions of dropout on drug use, interactions
with social sanctions and poverty status 177

Table A- 27. Predictors of delinquency, 1997 179

Table A- 28. Predictors of drug use, 1997 184

List of Figures

Figure 2-1: Conceptual diagram of delinquency and drug use causing dropout ... 12

Figure 2-2: Conceptual diagram of alternative explanations for delinquency, drug use, and dropout ... 16

Figure 4-1: Proportion of dropouts, by survey year ... 52

Figure 4-2: Proportion of dropouts, by survey year and poverty status ... 53

Figure 4-3: Predicted probability of dropout from hybrid random effects model, by delinquency ... 61

Figure 4-4: Predicted probability of dropout from hybrid random effects model, by drug use ... 63

Figure 4-5: Predicted probability of dropout from hybrid random effects model, by delinquency, arrest, and poverty status ... 76

Acknowledgements

In 2000, I came on board as a research assistant for a project headed up by John Echeverry at George Washington University. John introduced me to the process of research and helped to lay a solid foundation for research habits that have stuck with me in my professional career. He sparked an interest in the topics of substance abuse and risky behaviors that is partly reflected in this work. Tragically, John has since passed away and was never able to read or comment on any part of this book.

For this particular project, I am indebted to several individuals. First, I am indebted to Karl Alexander. His feedback on my writing always hit the nail on the head, and he showed me how to turn complex statistical models into a story about individual lives, an art that I hope will one day come as easily to me as it does to him. I would also like to thank Steve Plank for introducing me to the NLSY97. I would also like to thank Lingxin Hao for replying to my many e-mail questions and welcoming my many unscheduled office visits to ask for advice on methods. I should have never told other graduate students that her courses were too hard!

This research was supported by a grant from the American Educational Research Association which receives its funds for its "AERA Grants Program" from the National Science Foundation and the National Center for Education Statistics of the Institute of Education Sciences (U.S. Department of Education) under NSF Grant #DRL-0634035. The opinions found within this book are my own and do not necessarily reflect those of the granting agencies.

Finally, I would like to thank Leo Balk, of LFB Scholarly Press, and Marilyn McShane and Frank P. Williams, III, editors of the Recent Scholarship in Criminal Justice Series, for their editorial advice and for shepherding this book through the publication process.

CHAPTER 1

Drug Use, Delinquency, and Dropout

INTRODUCTION

Graduating from high school is an important developmental task that marks the transition out of adolescence and into adulthood. Over the past several years, several reports have suggested that only two thirds of youth graduate within four years of entering high school, and that the odds of graduating from high school for black and Hispanic youth barely break 50/50 (Barton 2005; Greene and Winters 2006; Swanson and Chaplin 2003).[1] Dropout rates remain high (Stillwell 2010). The consequences of dropping out of high school have been well documented (Coley 1995; Rumberger 1987). In an economy that places a high value on education and where few jobs exist for those without a high school diploma, high school dropouts face unemployment, welfare dependency, and imprisonment. In addition to being costly to the individual high school dropout, a youth's decision not to continue with his or her education is also expensive for the rest of society in terms of forgone tax revenues and increased expenditures on a variety of social programs, from remedial education to criminal justice. Given all of these negative consequences, it is particularly pressing to understand why youth drop out of school.

One factor that is strongly related to a youth's decision to drop out of high school is participation in problem or deviant behavior, including delinquency and drug use. However, while few would dispute that delinquency and drug use are associated with dropout, there is a great deal of debate as to whether delinquency and drug use actually lead to dropout. While some studies suggest that delinquency and drug use influence a youth's decision about whether to stay in school, other studies suggest that delinquency and drug use are unimportant for dropout once other factors related to dropout, such as school failure, are taken into consideration. This study is motivated by this lack of consensus among prior studies on the effects of delinquency and drug use on dropout. In this study, I seek to address three limitations of prior studies that may account for these contradictory findings. (1) Prior studies have not seriously considered an alternative explanation for why youth who participate in delinquency and drug use drop out, specifically, that youth *self-select* into delinquency, drug use, and dropout. (2) Prior studies have not examined whether the effects of delinquency and drug use on dropout are different for youth from different social classes. (3) Prior studies have not examined whether social sanctions—such as getting into trouble at school or with the law—moderate the effects of delinquency and drug use on dropout.

BACKGROUND

Delinquency and drug use among youth have been declining since the 1990s (Johnston et al. 2008; Snyder 2008). However, these behaviors are no less of a concern to parents, educators, and the public. This is because delinquency and drug use are believed to put youth at risk for a wide variety of deleterious outcomes both in adolescence and in adulthood. In the short-term, delinquency and drug use have been linked to academic failure (Farnworth, Schweinhart, and Berrueta-Clement 1985; Tremblay et al. 1992), school disengagement (Liska and Reed 1985), early sexual activitiy and teenage pregnancy (Mensch and Kandel 1992), and living independently of one's parents (Krohn, Lizotte, and Perez 1997). In the long-term, delinquency and drug use have been linked to lower levels of educational and occupational attainment (Tanner, Davies, and O'Grady 1999), higher levels of depression (Hagan 1997), divorce, and a greater risk of alcohol and drug dependence (White, Bates, and Labouvie 1998).

One possible consequence of delinquency and drug use is dropping out of high school. Indeed, perhaps no factor is as strongly related to a youth's decision to drop out of high school as is participation in delinquency and drug use (Bachman, O'Malley, and Johnston 1978; Elliott and Voss 1974; Mensch and Kandel 1988). However, what is not so clear is *why* youth who engage in delinquency and drug use are more likely to also drop out of high school. The common sense explanation—one that is familiar to many parents of teenagers—is that delinquency and problem behavior puts youth on the path to dropping out of high school. However, the evidence that delinquency and drug use lead to dropout is actually quite thin. While some studies indicate that delinquency and drug use do contribute to a youth's decision to drop out (Kaplan and Liu 1994; Mensch and Kandel 1988), other studies suggest that delinquency and drug use are not harmful to a youth's graduation prospects once other predictors of dropout, such as poor grades, low commitment to school, and weak bonds to family, are taken into account (Fagan and Pabon 1990; Krohn et al. 1995; McCaffery et al. 2010).

How can some studies show that delinquency and drug use lead to dropping out of high school at the same time that other studies show that problem behavior does not matter at all? Some have argued that these conflicting findings are evidence that an alternative explanation for why delinquency and drug use are related to dropout is required. More specifically, these authors argue that delinquency, drug use, and dropping out are all just manifestations of a general pattern of deviant or age-inappropriate behavior in a youth's life (Jessor and Jessor 1977; Newcomb and Bentler 1988). According to researchers who make this argument, rather than delinquency and drug use leading to dropout, youth *self-select* into all three behaviors. Youth who are dissatisfied with school are likely to rebel by engaging in delinquency and drug use. These youth are also likely to drop out of school, but not because of delinquency or drug use. The decision to drop out simply represents a process of disengagement from school that began before delinquency or drug use. It is therefore not surprising, according to these authors, that prior studies have not all found that delinquency and drug use lead to dropping out as they have not controlled for all of the factors that might account for delinquency and drug use as well as dropping out.

Others researchers have taken a more nuanced approach to explaining these divergent findings. While not ruling out the possibility that an alternative explanation may be at play, some have argued that the disagreement among prior studies may reflect the fact that they look at different types of dropouts, and that delinquency and drug use are not associated with dropping out among certain subgroups (Janosz, Le Blanc, and Boulerice 1998). In other words, there may be certain characteristics that moderate the influence of delinquency and drug use on dropout. For example, Janosz et al. (1998) argue that some dropouts are characterized by poor psychosocial adjustment and problem behavior, whereas other dropouts are socially adjusted and show no problem behavior. This work underscores the importance of considering differences between dropouts when examining the relationship of delinquency and drug use to dropout.

In addition to psychosocial differences, dropouts can be differentiated on a much broader level in terms of social class. Not all dropouts fit the mold of the typical "at risk" youth. Some dropouts come from middle-class families and are doing average or even better than average in school. Moreover, research suggests that there may be different etiological paths to dropout for youth from different social classes. Streeter and Franklin (1991) found, for example, that while dropouts from middle-class families were doing better in school than average, they had more family and behavioral problems, felt more alienated from school, and were more likely to use drugs. Lower-class dropouts, on the other hand, were less involved in problem behavior and came from families that made less money and were not doing well academically. These findings suggest that delinquency and drug use may be part of the dropout process for middle-class youth but not for lower-class youth. Surprisingly little research has examined how the predictors of dropping out differ for middle-class and lower-class dropouts, and even fewer studies have examined these potential differences when it comes to delinquency and drug use. The lack of attention to differences between middle-class and lower-class dropouts, in addition to the failure to adequately address the possibility that youth self-select into all three behaviors, might explain the divergent findings of prior studies on the effects of delinquency and drug use on dropout.

A third but related issue that is difficult to ignore—especially when considering the possible role of social class—is what happens to youth as a result of their participation in delinquency and drug use. Delinquency and drug use may not always lead to dropout. If delinquency and drug use lead to getting into trouble at school or with the law—such as being suspended from school or arrested—then youth may be more likely to drop out than if the behaviors go undetected or are not sanctioned. While there are theoretical reasons to believe that delinquency and drug use may lead to dropout even in the absence of sanctions, the failure to consider this possibility may lead to incorrect conclusions about the effects of delinquency and drug use. Moreover, given the class disparity in the likelihood of being sanctioned, it is especially important to examine the possible conditioning effect of sanctions separately for youth from different social classes. While lower-class youth may be more likely to be sanctioned, delinquency and drug use may lead to drop out for middle-class youth who are sanctioned, since they have more to loose.

Understanding whether delinquency and drug use lead to dropout is not just an academic debate but has important practical implications. The decision to drop out of high school is one of the most serious decisions a youth will ever make, since high school dropouts are likely to experience a wide array of problems, both immediately after leaving school as well as later in life. If delinquency and drug use lead to dropout, then dropout prevention strategies that focus on adolescent problem behaviors are likely to be effective in reducing dropout. If, on the other hand, delinquency and drug use are symptoms of much larger school, family, or individual problems, then strategies to reduce dropout would want to anticipate a wide array of adjustment problems in multiple domains and focus instead on the more central factors that give rise to delinquency, drug use, and dropout. Moreover, understanding whether delinquency and drug use are part of the etiology of dropout for some youth but not for others would make dropout prevention strategies more targeted and lead to a more nuanced understanding of multiple dropout processes.

In this study, I examine the effects of delinquency and drug use on high school dropout. My primary goal is to understand whether delinquency and drug use lead to dropout and, if so, for whom and under what conditions. I do this by paying particular attention to three critical issues that I have identified as weaknesses in the existing literature: the possibility of self-selection, differences between dropouts in terms of social class, and the limited attention to the processes—specifically social sanctions—that may link delinquency and drug use to dropout. To do this, I use recent, longitudinal data from the National Longitudinal Survey of Youth 1997 (NLSY97), which is sponsored by the U.S. Bureau of Labor Statistics. The NLSY97 is a nationally representative, longitudinal sample of just fewer than 9,000 youth who were born between 1980 and 1984. The NLSY97 contains information on youths' school enrollment, delinquency, and drug use measured annually.

In seeking to better understand the relationship between prior delinquency and prior drug use and later dropping out, this study addresses three specific research questions:

1. Do delinquency and drug use lead to dropout, or are delinquency and drug use themselves responsive to the same factors that cause dropout?
2. Do the effects of delinquency and drug use vary by type of dropout, specifically, for lower-class and middle-class dropouts?
3. Does what happens to youth as a result of delinquency and drug use—namely, whether they are arrested or have legal problems—affect whether delinquency and drug use lead to dropout?

I address the first research question in two ways. First, like prior researchers who have examined this topic, I employ a wide array of control variables designed to capture important differences between youth with different degrees of participation in delinquency and drug use and which may also predict dropout. The NLSY97 facilitates this through its particularly rich information collected from a variety of domains in youths' lives. Second, recognizing that some differences may be difficult or impossible to observe and include in my statistical models and may therefore pose a threat to causal inference, I employ models for panel data the address the possibility of selection on observed as well as certain types of *unobserved* differences. This modeling strategy will allow me to estimate the effects of delinquency and drug use on dropping out while controlling for *all* stable individual characteristics of youth, such as a tendency toward deviance, a desire to grow up quickly, or an early state of school disengagement. As such, it provides a significant improvement over prior studies and is a step toward understanding which explanation—cause or effect—for the link between delinquency and drug use and dropout is correct. I address the second research question by including interactions between delinquency (and drug use) and social class. Finally, delinquency and drug use are interacted with indicators of school suspension and arrest to determine whether the effects of delinquency and dropout depend on the reaction to delinquency and drug use.

CHAPTER 2

Causes of Dropout

DROPOUT: THE EXTENT OF THE PROBLEM, CONSEQUENCES, AND CAUSES

Extent of Dropping Out

Dropping out of high school is a serious educational and social problem that is costly to both the individual and to society (Rumberger 1987). The most widely cited dropout statistic is the status dropout rate, which is reported by the National Center for Education Statistics (NCES) of the U.S. Department of Education and is calculated using educational attainment data from the Current Population Survey (CPS) of the U.S. Census, which are derived from self-reports of school enrollment. The status dropout rate has long been accepted as the "official" dropout rate. The status dropout rate measures the number of individuals in a specific age range who are not in school and who have not completed a high school diploma or GED. GED holders are counted as graduates. Figures from the latest report show that in 2007, 8.7 percent of 16- to 24-year-olds were not enrolled in school and did not have a diploma, which is down from 14.6 in 1972(Cataldi et al. 2009). Therefore, the "official" dropout rate says that less than 10 percent of youth drop out of school and that the percentage of youth who drop out has been declining in recent decades.

However, in the last few years, a number of independent researchers have claimed that the dropout rate is much higher, particularly for black and Hispanic youth. Using data from the Common Core of Data (CCD), which is collected annually by NCES and contains administrative data on enrollment and diplomas that schools report to their districts, these researchers claim that only about two thirds of youth are graduating high school on time with a regular high school diploma (Barton 2003; Greene and Winters 2006; Miao and Haney 2004; Swanson and Chaplin 2003) and high school completion rates have actually been decreasing. According to one statistic (Swanson and Chaplin 2003), as few as two thirds of 9th graders complete high school with a regular diploma four years later. Graduation rates for students from historically disadvantaged minority groups are even lower. For black and Hispanic youth, according to these statistics, the odds of graduating high school within four years barely break the 50/50 mark.

How can these two dropout rates be so different? Warren and Halpern-Manners (2007) found that about half of the difference between the two statistics could be accounted for by the way in which they treat private high school graduate and GED holders. First, the CPS counts public and private high school graduates, whereas the CCD does not provide any information about private schools, which tend to have higher graduation rates. Second, the CPS counts both high school graduates and GED holders as graduates, whereas the CCD counts only high school diplomas. The other half of the difference was explained by the fact that CPS respondents misrepresent their children's enrollment status in high school either due to social desirability or to confusion about their child's enrollment status. They conclude that the CCD is a better measure of high school dropout. However, the main issue might be that these measures are conceptually different. While the CPS measure is a measure of educational attainment (by including GED holders), the CCD measure is a measure of how well the educational system is doing in graduating students. What is clear is that regardless of how many students drop out, levels of dropout are higher than we would want. Moreover, as reviewed in the next section, these high levels of dropping out are costly to both the individual dropout and to the rest of society.

Consequences of Dropping Out

The decision to drop out of school is one of the most important decisions a youth has to make, since a dropout is likely to face a number of difficulties, both immediately after dropping out as well as later in life. The negative consequences of dropping out of high school have been well documented. Nearly one half of all high school dropouts ages 16 to 24 are jobless (Sum et al. 2003), and high school dropouts earn about $9,245 less per year than high school graduates

(Doland 2001). Additionally, nearly half of all heads of households on welfare (Schwartz 1995) and 41 percent of prison inmates (Harlow 2003) are high school dropouts. Indeed, the adverse consequences of dropout apparently even extend to health outcomes. For example, high school dropouts are at a greater risk of being diagnosed with a lifetime alcohol use disorder (Crum et al. 1998), and dropouts are more likely to die early (defined as before their average life expectancy) than are those with a high school diploma (Alliance for Excellent Education 2003). Finally, as the college degree begins to replace the high school diploma as a necessary ingredient for success in American (although it does not guarantee success), a high school diploma also serves as a gateway to postsecondary education. Given all of these negative consequences, it is important to understand why youth drop out of school.

Causes of Dropping Out

Rumberger's (2004) overview of individual and institutional perspectives on dropout is a good place to begin. The individual perspective focuses on identifying risk factors for dropout associated with the individual youth, such as their attitudes and behaviors. Such individual-level risk factors include school performance (Bachman, Green, and Wirtanen 1971; Ekstrom et al. 1986), and school disengagement (Alexander, Entwisle, and Kabbani 2001; Archambault et al. 2009; Janosz et al. 2008; Wehlage and Rutter 1986). Dropouts are also less popular among their peers than graduates (Parker and Asher 1987; Staff and Kreager 2007) and are more likely to have a history of frequent residential and school mobility (Rumberger 1995; Swanson and Schneider 1999). Taking on adult roles and responsibilities while still in high school (or so called "accelerated role transitions") is also associated with dropping out, including becoming a parent (Mott and Marsiglio 1985; Pirog and Magee 1997) and working long hours at a job (Goldschmidt and Wang 1999; Marsh 1991; Staff and Lee 2007; Warren and Lee 2003).

The individual perspective views dropout as a long-term process of disengagement from school. Applying such a life course perspective, several studies of dropout have examined predictors from elementary school, in some cases as far back as first grade (Alexander, Entwisle, and Horsey 1997; Alexander et al. 2001; Cairns, Cairns, and Neckerman 1989; Ensminger and Slusarcick 1992). These studies generally find that risk factors measured early in students' academic careers are just as important as those measured later for predicting whether they will eventually drop out of school. For example, in their longitudinal sample of about 800 Baltimore students followed since first grade, Alexander et al. (2001) found that academic performance and engagement measured in the 1st grade predicted dropout almost as well as similar measures from middle school and the first year of high school.

The second perspective, the institutional perspective, is concerned with the context of youth's home and school. Such contextual risk factors include low socioeconomic status (Ekstrom et al. 1986; Rumberger 1983) and single- or step-parent family status (Astone and McLanahan 1994; Teachman, Paasch, and Carver 1996). A large body of research focuses on how the characteristics of the schools that youth attend are related to dropout. Several of the individual-level risk factors for dropout are also related to dropout at the aggregate or school-level. Youth who attend lower SES schools are more likely to drop out than youth who attend higher SES schools (Bryk and Thum 1989; Mayer 1991; Rumberger 1995; Rumberger and Thomas 2000). School resources are also related to dropout. For example, youth are also more likely to drop out if they attend schools with higher student-teacher ratios (McNeal 1997; Rumberger 1995; Rumberger and Thomas 2000). School structure is another characteristic of schools that is related to dropout. Urban schools have higher dropout rates than suburban schools, and public schools have higher dropout rates than Catholic schools and private schools (Bryk and Thum 1989; Coleman and Hoffer 1987; Evans and Schwab 1995; Neal 1997; Rumberger and Thomas 2000; Sander and Krautmann 1995). Finally, school processes are also related to dropout. Schools use administrative procedures such as age cut-offs, grade point average minimums, and attendance regulations to "push out" students with a history of academic and behavioral problems (Elliott and Voss 1974; Gottfredson and Gottfredson 1985; Jackson 1983; Mann 1987; Riehl 1999).

Delinquency, Drug Use, and Dropout

Another factor that is strongly related to dropping out is participation in deviant behavior, including delinquency and drug use. Several studies have documented that youth who eventually drop out of high school are more involved in delinquency and drug use while they are still in school than youth who eventually graduate (Ekstrom et al. 1986; Elliott and Voss 1974; Hathaway, Reynolds, and Monachesi 1969; Mensch and Kandel 1988; Thornberry, Moore, and Christenson 1985), For example, in their longitudinal study of 2,617 students from eight schools in California, Elliott and Voss (1974) found that, while in school, dropouts had higher rates of police contacts and self-reported delinquency than graduates. Similarly, Bachman et al. (1978) found that the young men in the Youth and Transition study who later became high school dropouts were more involved in cigarette smoking, alcohol use, and delinquent behavior in high school than high school graduates. Analyzing data from High School and Beyond (HS&B), Ekstrom et al. (1986) found that dropouts were more likely to have school-related delinquency and disciplinary problems in their sophomore year of high school. Therefore, involvement in delinquency and drug use appear to be precursors to dropping out of high school. As we shall see, however, it is not clear exactly *why* youth who are involved in delinquency and drug use are also likely to drop out of school.

A TALE OF TWO VIEWS

The Traditional View: Delinquency and Drug Use Cause Dropping Out

While it is clear that youth who participate in delinquency and drug use are more likely to drop out of school, there are two very different views on why this is the case. One view is that delinquency and drug use cause dropping out of school. Several different theoretical perspectives have been offered to support this causal explanation. For example, Mensch and Kandel (1988) speculate that drug use reinforces association with other youth who use drugs, who encourage disinterest in academics and skipping school, both of which lead to dropping out. McCluskey et al. (2002) argue that delinquency and drug use cause youth to take on adult roles, such as parenthood and moving out of their parents' house, prematurely, which in turn leads to dropping out. Regarding drug use specifically, Newcomb and Bentler (1988) take a different tack, pointing out that chronic drug use can have psychoactive effects on cognitive, affective, and behavioral processes, which may impair the ability to function in the role of student. Figure 2-1 presents a conceptual diagram of the various explanations that have been offered for why delinquency and drug use would lead to dropping out of high school.

Figure 2-1. Conceptual diagram of delinquency and drug use causing dropout

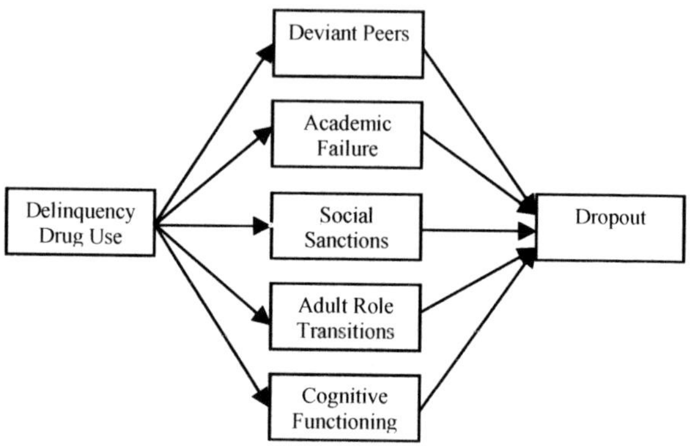

Finn (1989) has developed two models of the dropout process that posit a causal and more general role for delinquency and drug use. Finn's first model, the frustration-self-esteem model, argues that poor school performance leads a youth to become frustrated and embarrassed, which in turn leads to low self-esteem. Low self-esteem causes a youth to reject school, which they view as the source of their negative feelings. This rejection of school may take the form of delinquency, drug use, or disruptive behavior in the classroom, which a student believes will increase their self-esteem while providing success in another arena—specifically, rebellious behavior. According to the frustration-self-esteem model, delinquency and problem behavior escalate and negatively affect school performance until the student eventually drops out.

While the frustration-self-esteem model focuses on internal psychological processes, Finn's (1989) second model of dropout—the participation-identification model—focuses on a youth's behavioral and emotional involvement with school. According to this model, students who fail to develop a sense of identification with school will drop out. The development of a sense of identification stems from participation in classroom and school activities, which fosters academic success, promotes a sense of belonging and valuing school-related goals, and increases future involvement in school. The failure to participate in these activities leads to poor academic performance, a lack of support and encouragement to continue participating in school, and emotional withdrawal from school. As the student gets older, attempts at withdrawal manifest themselves as delinquency and problem behavior, including truancy and disruptive behavior. As the attention of teachers and school officials becomes focused on the problem behavior, and as suspensions and other disciplinary practices prevent the student from further participating in school activities, dropping out is likely. The participation-identification model views dropping out as the most extreme form of non-participation in school.

When examined more closely, both the frustration-self-esteem and participation-identification models are similar. Both models view dropping out as a long-term process of disengagement from school. Both models also view disengagement as the immediate impetus to dropping out. However, both models also view delinquency and drug use as causes of dropping out. Therefore, both the frustration-self-esteem and participation-identification models posit a cyclical relationship between delinquency and drug use and school disengagement in the dropout process, which eventually culminates in leaving school.

There is some evidence to support the claim that delinquency and drug use are causally related to dropping out of school. Several studies have examined whether delinquency (Ellickson et al. 1998; Fagan and Pabon 1990; Krohn et al. 1995) and drug use (Fagan and Pabon 1990; Friedman, Glickmand, and Utada 1983; Krohn et al. 1995; Mensch and Kandel 1988; Newcomb and Bentler 1988) lead to dropping out of school once other predictors of dropping out, such as socioeconomic status and school performance are taken into account. For example, Friedman, Glickmand, and Utada (1983) controlled for over 20 demographic, personal, and family factors related to dropout and still found that the severity of a youth's drug use predicted their failure to graduate from high school. Similarly, Mensch and Kandel (1988) found the use of licit and illicit drugs increased the risk of dropping out over and above risk factors for drug use and dropout. They controlled for a large number of factors predictive of dropping out, including socioedemographic background, adult role transitions, other deviant behaviors, and individual attributes. Their finding led them to conclude that "Since various factors that could determine both drug use and dropping out of school were controlled for in multivariate analyses, the results lead to the conclusion that dropping out is a partial function of drug use itself" (111).

However, not all research supports the traditional view that delinquency and drug use cause dropping out. For example, Fagon and Pabon (1990) found that delinquency and drug use added little explanatory power to models of dropout that included measures of social bonds to family, school, peers, and community. They concluded, "Although delinquency and substance use are more frequent and serious among school dropouts, knowledge of these behaviors adds little to explanations of dropout rates among inner-city youths" (338). However, their cross-sectional data could not distinguish delinquency and drug use that occurred before dropping out from delinquency and drug use that occurred after dropping out. Moreover, since their sample was one of inner-city youth, the generalizability of their findings is limited to inner-city adolescents.

Using longitudinal data from the Rochester Youth Development Study (RYDS), Krohn et al. (1995) examined dropping out as both a cause and consequence of delinquency and drug use while controlling for family and school variables identified by prior research to be predictive of all three behaviors. Krohn and his colleagues found that delinquency did not increase the risk of dropping out controlling for demographic, family, and school variables. Underclass status, GPA, commitment to school, and expectations about going to college were more important than prior delinquency for explaining dropout. The non-significant finding for delinquency led them to conclude: "It appears that dropping out of school, the use of drugs, and participation in delinquent behavior might form a constellation of problematic behaviors that are, in part, caused by dissatisfaction with school" (182).

A number of more recent studies have produced similar results (Bachman 2008; Flisher et al. 2010; McCaffery et al. 2010). For example, using data from the Monitoring the Future study, Bachman and his colleagues (2008) found that while adolescents who used drugs were more likely to drop out, most types of drug use had no or at most modest effects on school completion once predictors of both behaviors were taken into account. Because academic failure predicted drug use, dropout, and delinquency, Bachman et al. concluded that both behaviors were part of a much wider problem behavior syndrome. In short, these findings suggest that the reason why youth who are involved in drug use are also prone to dropout has *little or nothing to do* with their drug use or delinquency.

Therefore, while early delinquency and drug use are strongly related to eventually dropping out of school, the common sense explanation that delinquency and drug use are *causally* related to dropping out is not necessarily fully supported by the existing literature on the topic. In fact, some studies suggest that the delinquency and drug use are actually *spuriously* related to dropout. Table A-1 provides a summary of the various studies that have been conducted on this topic, including the data sets, the specific measures of delinquency, drug use, and dropout employed, and the results of the study.

An Alternative View

The lack of consensus in prior studies has led some researchers to take a different approach to explaining the relationship among delinquency, drug use, and dropout, arguing that delinquency, drug use, and dropout are symptoms of much larger problems in a youth's life. There are two predominant explanations that have emerged in the literature on this topic for why this would be the case: problem behavior theory and precocious development theory. According to problem behavior theory (Donovan and Jessor 1985; Jessor and Jessor 1977), problem behaviors, such as problem drinking, illicit drug use, delinquency, and precocious sexual activity, co-occur in adolescence as part of a "syndrome" of problem behavior. The Jessors argue that the intercorrelations among problem behaviors can be accounted for by an underlying tendency toward deviance or nonconventionality caused by a common set of social psychological antecedents. Moreover, the undlerying nonconventionality is assumed to by relatively stable over time. Problem behaviors are functionally equivalent and serve the purpose of gaining adult status by the adolescent. According to the Jessors, dropping out is itself a problem behavior and represents another attempt by the youth at ganing adult status. Therefore, from the perspective of problem behavior theory, delinquency and drug use are not important causes of dropout; rather, all three behaviors are symptoms of an underlying deviance proneness.

Another perspective which has been commonly employed is precocious development theory (Newcomb and Bentler 1988). According to precocious development theory, drug use, delinquency, and other forms of adolescent deviance are likely to be associated with dropout because they reflect an underlying "psuedomaturity" that propels youth into adult roles prematurely. According to Newcomb and Bentler, precocious youth "tend to bypass or circumvent the typical maturational sequence of school, work, and marriage and become engaged in adult roles of jobs and family prematurely, without the necessary growth and development to enhance success with these roles" (1988:35-36). Newcomb and Bentler argue that youth who engage in precocious behaviors may be characterized by an inability to delay gratification, and that "(a)s a result, the rewarding aspects of adulthood are sought and coveted (i.e., drug use, sexual involvement), while avoiding the more difficult tasks of adulthood that would be gained with experience and maturity (i.e., responsibility, forethought)" (1988:37-38). Delinquency and drug use are generally perceived as more mature by peers because they signal independence from adult authority. Dropping out of high school may be also one manifestation of pseudomaturity, since youth who desire to grow up quickly are unlikely to find the youth-oriented environment of high school compatible with their more adult lifestyles. According to Newcomb and Bentler, psuedomaturity is driven by a difficulty delaying gratification. Therefore, precocious development theory has been used to argue that delinquency, drug use, and dropout are related because delinquent and drug using youth are too impulsive to refrain from rebellious behavior and to put off engaging in adult lifestyles until after graduation from high school.

Figure 2-2. Conceptual diagram of alternative explanations for delinquency, drug use, and dropout

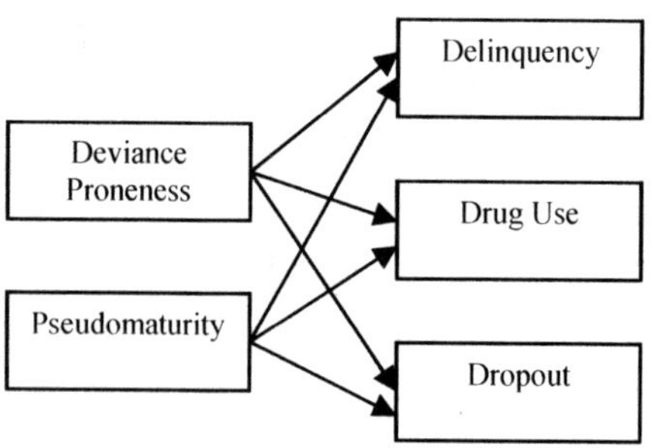

Problem behavior theory and precocious development theory differ somewhat in their explanation of the underlying mechanism driving

youth to participate in delinquency, drug use, and dropout. For example, the syndrome of problem behaviors that underlie problem behavior theory are uniformly considered socially undesirable. Precocious development theory, however, views the syndrome of behaviors as not necessarily deviant but simply age-inappropriate. Many of the behaviors that constitute the syndrome are actually considered socially desirable for adults. For example, working and engaging in sexual relationships are not behaviors (like criminal activity) that are considered deviant. Rather, they are behaviors that are considered socially desirable for adults but not for youth. But despite their differences, both theories maintain that delinquency and drug use are unimportant for a youths' decision to drop out. Figure 2-2 presents a conceptual diagram of these alternative explanations for delinquency, drug use, and dropout.

Indeed, there is some evidence to support the specific perspectives offered by problem behavior and precocious development theories. The first line of evidence comes from studies that show that a wide array of problem behaviors can be accounted for by a single underlying trait. These studies used factor analysis to examine the intercorrelations among multiple problem behaviors in order to determine whether there is a single tendency towards deviance among adolescents (Donovan and Jessor 1985; Donovan, Jessor, and Costa 1988; Mott and Haurin 1988; Osgood et al. 1988). These studies generally suggest that a single construct explains most of the covariation in problem behaviors. For example, Osgood et al. (1988) found that a "general deviance" construct accounted for virtually all of the covariation among alcohol use, marijuana use, other illicit drug use, dangerous driving, and criminal behavior. Although none of these studies include a measure of dropout specifically, they do provide some credence to the claim that an underlying syndrome may account for participation in a diverse array of problem behaviors.

The second line of evidence comes from studies that have attempted to identify the variables that mediate the effects of delinquency and drug use on dropout (Kaplan and Liu 1994; McCluskey et al. 2002). Some of these studies have found that the inclusion of measures of adult role participation mediates the effects of delinquency and drug use on dropout. For example, Kaplan and Lui (1994; McCluskey et al. 2002) found that while drug use had effects on dropout once a host of risk factors for drug use and dropout were controlled, the addition of measures of adult role transitions in the next year—including marriage, pregnancy, and having children—rendered the effects of drug use on dropout non-significant. While this result could be interpreted as evidence of a mediating effect, the high correlation between drug use and adult role transitions and the fact that adult roles explained the effects of drug use on dropout can also be interpreted as evidence of an underlying pseudomaturity (Janosz and Le Blanc 1997).

A third source of evidence on this issue, and one that is most germane to the problem of dropout, comes from studies examining the relationship of "off-time" transitions to adult roles and delinquency, drug use, and dropping out of high school. Krohn, Lizotte, and Perez (1997) found that early use of alcohol and drugs was associated not only with dropping out of high school but also with teenage pregnancy (among females), getting someone else pregnant (among males), and living independently of parents or guardians prematurely. High school employment—another adult role—is also associated with participation in delinquency and drug use (Bachman and Schulenberg 1993). Moreover, other studies indicate that taking on adult roles, such as teenage pregnancy (Mott and Marsiglio 1985) and employment, are strongly associated with dropping out. Youth who work or have children may already be dissatisfied with school, and teenage pregnancy and intensive work may be better thought of as symptoms of bigger problems rather than causes of dropping out. These findings are consistent with precocious development theory, since one commonality to all of the behaviors is that they represent a drive by youth to gain independence from adult authority and to hasten the transition to adult roles. Like teenage pregnancy, high school employment, and high school dropout, participation in delinquency and drug use may be just one more sign or symptom of a youth's desire to leave adolescence behind.

To sum up, one fact is not in dispute: youth who are involved in early delinquency and drug use are more likely to drop out of high school than youth who are not. What *is* in dispute, however, is whether delinquency and drug use are causes of dropping out of school. The results of studies examining the issue have been mixed, with some studies inferring or claiming a causal relationship and others indicating that delinquency and drug use are not important contributors to dropout. These divergent findings have led some researchers to propose alternative explanations for why youth who are involved in delinquency and drug use are likely to drop out, in particular, that all three behaviors are symptoms of an underlying constellation of deviant or age-inappropriate behaviors. As such, the majority of studies on this topic have focused their attention on trying to assess which explanation—delinquency and drug use cause dropping out or delinquency and drug use are part of a "general deviance" syndrome – is correct. Other researchers, however, have taken a different approach.

DELINQUENCY, DRUG USE, AND DIFFERENT TYPES OF DROPOUTS

We have already seen that some researchers have attempted to explain the conflicting findings of prior studies by arguing that delinquency and drug use are evidence of a pattern of problematic or age-inappropriate behavior in a youth's life. There is, however, a second, more nuanced approach that has been employed to explain this lack of consensus. Janosz and Le Blanc (1997) argue that, in addition to the possibility that youth self-select into all three behaviors based on an underlying motivation to engage in deviance or to grow up quickly, one reason why past research on the effects of delinquency and drug use on dropout has yielded contradictory findings is because it has not taken into account the differences between, or "heterogeneity" of, dropouts. They used data from a sample of white, French-speaking students in Montreal to examine whether delinquency and drug use predicted two types of dropouts: "quiet dropouts" and "maladjusted dropouts." Quiet dropouts were dropouts who were committed to school and did not engage in problem behavior in class. Maladjusted dropouts showed a high level of school maladjustment, indicating problem behaviors. Janosz and Le Blanc found that delinquency and drug use predicted maladjusted dropout but were negatively associated with quiet dropout. They suggested that the findings of prior studies depended largely on the distribution of the types of dropouts—quiet or maladjusted— included in the sample. This study underscores the importance of examining subgroup differences among dropouts in the effects of delinquency and drug use as a way of reconciling the findings of previous studies. With the exception of Janosz et al.'s study, the heterogeneity of dropouts has not been addressed when examining the effects of delinquency and drug use on dropout.

Social Class and Dropouts: Another Source of Heterogeneity

Dropout is strongly related to social class, as measured by both parental income and parental education (Ekstrom et al. 1986; Rumberger 1983). However, not all youth who leave school before graduation fit the typical mold of an "at-risk" youth—that is, not all dropouts are failing in school and come from lower-class families. Youth from middle-class families also drop out of school. Streeter and Franklin (1991) examined differences between lower-income dropouts and middle-class dropouts. While these two groups of dropouts differed in terms of socioeconomic factors, there were also psychological, family, and academic differences. Lower-class dropouts were characterized by lower family incomes, minority group status, and lower levels of academic achievement. The problems of low-income dropouts were "mainly socioeconomic and academic in nature" (211). On the other hand, middle-class dropouts were predominantly white, had higher incomes, and scored on average a grade level above their current grade on achievement tests at the time of dropout. In terms of family differences, middle-class dropouts tended to perceive less bonding and support at home, were more likely to be involved in drug use, and had higher levels of depression and thought more about suicide than lower-class dropouts. They also reported being more disengaged from school, despite their higher GPAs and achievement test scores. Overall, therefore, lower-class dropouts seemed to have left high school because they were poor and having academic problems; middle-class dropouts, on the other hand, seemed to have left school because of family dysfunction, a dislike of school, and involvement in problem behavior, including drug use.

In the context of the current problem, Streeter and Franklin's (1991) findings suggest that it is important to examine the effects of delinquency and drug use separately for middle-class and lower-class youth. However, exactly how this dynamic plays out for youth from different social classes remains uncertain. According to Sampson and Laub's (1997) cumulative disadvantage theory, delinquency and drug use will have greater effects on dropout for lower-class than for middle-class adolescents. Individuals in poor urban settings have less of an opportunity buffer, and early deficits and disadvantages are likely to pile up and amplify current problems. For these individuals, delinquency and problem behaviors restrict future opportunities in conventional domains (e.g., stable employment) while at the same time fostering resentment of conventional activities and encouraging membership is deviant subcultures that provide alternative opportunities. Moreover, lower-class adolescents also have little social capital to bargain their way out of stigmatization from having engaged in delinquency and problem behaviors. For example, a lower-class student who is suspended from school for being disruptive may not have parents who are able or willing (e.g., because of having to work or discomfort about dealing with school personnel, who likely have more education) to go to school and persuade school officials to impose a less harsh sentence. The suspension would result in further attention of the student's attachment to school.

The situation works very differently for middle-class parents, according to Sampson and Laub (1997). Advantaged positions provide continuity in social resources because individuals are more motivated to avoid negative life events that could jeopardize their incumbency in middle-class roles (e.g., being fired) and better able to establish binding ties to conventional lines of adult activity. For these reasons, legal sanctions are better able to deter middle-class individuals from subsequent offending. Furthermore, the parents of middle-class adolescents possess the personal ties and resources necessary to bargain their child's way out of punishments, such as school suspension, expulsion and even criminal charges. Put simply, a lower-class family provides fewer second chances and opportunities for mistakes than do middle-class families. According to Jessor, Donovan, and Costa (1991): "Contexts of poverty and social disorganization are obviously less likely than middle-class contexts to provide resources for overcoming a history of problem behavior, or to make 'second chances' available, that is, to be 'forgiving' in the sense of maintaining open opportunity despite previous problem behavior involvement" (1991:289).

However, one might, based on Streeter and Franklin's findings, expect that delinquency and drug use would be more important for dropout among middle-class dropouts than among lower-class dropouts. This idea finds support in disadvantage saturation theory (Hannon 2003). According to disadvantage saturation, delinquency and drug use are unlikely to lead to dropout for lower-class youth because lower-class youth are already at a high risk of dropout. Hannon (2003) describes disadvantage saturation: "At some point, the level of disadvantage could reach a point of saturation at which the youth has little left to lose in terms of opportunities for the future"

(578). The basic idea behind disadvantage saturation is that lower-class youth face so many obstacles to high school graduation--including socioeconomic problem and academic difficulties—that delinquency and drug use cannot have an independent effect on their decision to drop out. Lower-class youth are likely to drop out of school, anyway. Dropping out for lower-class youth seems to be the result of socioeconomic and academic difficulties, not of problem behavior.

The situation is somewhat different for middle-class youth, however. Most middle-class youth are on the path to graduating from high school and many middle-class parents even expect that their children will go to college. Since most middle-class youth do not face the same socioeconomic and academic difficulties faced by lower-class youth, there is more of an opportunity for delinquency and drug use to influence their decision to stay in school. Therefore, disadvantage saturation theory predicts that delinquency and drug use will lead to dropout for middle-class youth.

Indeed, there is some evidence to support the disadvantage saturation perspective on the effects of delinquency and drug use on dropout. Using data from the NLSY79, Hannon (2003) found that delinquency, getting in trouble at school for misbehavior, and getting arrested were related to lower educational attainment for youth whose family income was above the poverty line but not for those whose income was below the poverty line. Hannon took these findings as support for disadvantage saturation: "It appears that poverty and its multitude of associated setbacks make school infractions and problem with the law less important for determining educational attainment" (588).

THE REACTION TO DELINQUENCY AND DRUG USE

One factor that is impossible to ignore, especially when considering the possible role played by social class, is what happens to youth as a result of delinquency and drug use. The idea that delinquency and drug use lead to dropout is predicated on the assumption that these behaviors cause problems in a youth's life. Delinquency and drug use are associated with disciplinary problems and responses. Numerous studies have documented that being suspended from school or being arrested (De Li 1999; Hirschfield 2009; Sweeten 2006) are associated with dropping out of school. For example, using data from the HS&B study, Ekstrom et al (1986) found that eventual dropouts had more school-related discipline problems in their sophomore year of high school than did eventual graduates.   While existing theoretical explanations do not necessarily predicate the effects of delinquency and drug use on arrest, the failure to consider this issue could lead to erroneous conclusions about the effects of delinquency and drug use and may also account for the conflicting findings of prior studies.

Moreover, the fact that the likelihood of being suspended or arrested is greater for lower-class youth makes it extremely important to examine the role played by school suspension and arrest for youth from different social classes.   Students who receive free lunch or who have a father who is unemployed are overrepresented in school office referrals and suspension, and their punishments are more severe (Skiba, Peterson, and Williams 1997; Wu et al. 1982).   Lower-class youth are also more likely to get arrested, and there is evidence that social class plays a role in arrest decisions (Sampson 1986; Sealock and Simpson 1998).   Police are more likely to patrol neighborhoods where lower-class youth live, lower-class youth are more likely to hang out on the streets where they can be seen, and they are more likely to be picked up and questioned by the police.   Discrimination against lower-class youth in the justice system and possibly in school discipline makes these experiences more common for lower-class youth.

Yet, consistent with the viewpoint of disadvantage saturation, these experiences may not lead to dropout for lower-class youth.   Lower-class youth may already be viewed by society and even view themselves as deviant.   The acquisition of a deviant label from being arrested is unlikely to change the way that these youth view themselves or the way in which others view them.   However, middle-class youth are generally not considered by society to be deviant.   Therefore, they have a great deal to lose from the application of a deviant label.   If a middle-class youth engages in delinquency, being arrested or suspended for that delinquency is likely to lead to a decided shift in self-image and in the way that others view the youth.   Middle-class youth may ultimately come to view school authority as hostile. Therefore, engaging in delinquency and the punishment that follows may have more of an effect on dropout.

Therefore, while some researchers have argued that the lack of agreement in the literature on delinquency, drug use, and dropout stems from an underlying syndrome of problem behaviors, others claim that it has to do, at least partially, with the fact that dropouts are a heterogeneous group, and delinquency and drug use may not be part of the dropout process of all types of dropouts. One salient source of heterogeneity may be social class. As demonstrated by Streeter and Franklin (1991) (and as will be replicated in this study), middle-class dropouts have higher levels of problem behavior than lower-class dropouts, and there is some evidence to suggest that being sanctioned for deviant behavior matters more for middle-class youth than for lower-class youth. Differences in the social class composition of samples used by prior studies may partially account for the lack of agreement in their findings. It may be a mistake to investigate the relationship between prior delinquency and prior drug use and later dropping out without distinguishing middle-class dropouts from dropouts who fit the more traditional mold of an "at-risk" youth. Delinquency and drug use may be more part of the dropout process for middle-class dropouts than for lower-class dropouts.

MOVING THE RESEARCH FORWARD

To date, there is no answer to the seemingly simple question: Do delinquency and drug use lead to dropping out of high school? While some researchers purport to show a "causal" effect of delinquency and drug use on dropout, other researchers have found that delinquency and drug use can be explained by the same factors that also explain dropping out—that is, that the relationship is spurious. Two explanations have surfaced for explaining these contradictory findings. One is that delinquency and drug use are manifestations of bigger problems in a youth's life, such as a tendency to engage in deviance or an inability to delay gratification, which are also causes of dropout. A second approach has been to consider the differences between dropouts and how these might be related to participation in delinquency and drug use.

Janosz et al. (1998) took a step in the right direction by examining differences between dropouts in terms of their levels of psychosocial adjustment. However, while Janosz et al.'s study underscores the importance of examining subgroup differences between dropouts in the effect of delinquency and drug use, one weakness of their study is that the correlation between delinquency and maladjusted dropout may still not be causal. Differences in association do not imply differences in effects. Since maladjusted dropouts are already exhibiting problem behavior in class, an alternative explanation is that delinquency predicts maladjusted dropout because both behaviors represent a general tendency toward deviance or age-inappropriate behavior. These authors did not control for factors that are related to delinquency and drug use as well as to dropping out. In fact, Janosz and his colleagues note: "At this point, the goal of our research was not to model the differential influence and etiology of drug use and delinquency according to the different types of dropouts. This will be our next step, and to do so, more careful attention will have to be put on the potential controlling factors" (14). Therefore, a careful examination of the effects of delinquency and drug use on dropping out, controlling for the possibility of self-selection and examining the relationship separately for different types of dropouts, is necessary to advance the literature on this topic.

There are several ways to advance research on this topic. First, studies need to take seriously the possibility that youth are self-selected into all three behaviors. One reason why prior studies disagree with each other may be that they have not done an adequate job of testing the alternative view that delinquency and drug use are simply effects of the "real" causes of dropping out. Indeed, there is good reason to take seriously the alternative explanation that youth are self-selected into delinquency, drug use, and dropping out. First, many of the causes of dropping out are also causes of delinquency and drug use. For example, youth often engage in delinquency and drug use as a result of school failure (for a review, see Maguin and Loeber 1996) and school disengagement (Agnew and Petersen 1989; Steinberg and Avenevoli 1998; Steinberg, Brown, and Dornbusch 1996). Research has also found that coming from a single-parent family is related to both delinquency and drug use (Gove and Crutchfield 1982; Rebellon 2002), as are family processes, such as attachment to parents, involvement with parents, and parental supervision (Sampson and Laub 1993) Therefore, it is not unreasonable to suspect that youth who engage in delinquency and drug use are already at risk for dropping out of school even *before* they begin participating in delinquency and drug use. Such youth may already be less attached to school and performing poorly there, and they may be poorly bonded to family, which also increases the risk of dropping out. Rather than increasing their chances of leaving school, the emergence of delinquency and drug use in adolescence may be a symptom of much larger problems which also contribute to dropout.

Researchers who have studied this topic have recognized the possibility that youth are self-selected into delinquency, drug use, and dropping out. In fact, the question of whether the relationship among delinquency, drug use, and dropping out is causal or spurious has been the primary concern of prior studies on the topic. Prior studies have generally tried to address the possibility of self-selection by using multiple regression analysis to control for differences between youth that may predict all three behaviors by measuring these differences and including them in the models. However, such measures might not be adequate for capturing all of the relevant differences between youth. The main issue is that prior studies have relied on observational data to make claims about the causal effects of delinquency and drug use on dropping out. Unlike experiments, in which random assignment ensures that all individuals, on average, are equal with respect to all characteristics except the "treatment," (in this case, delinquency and drug use) observational research must approximate randomization by measuring differences and including them as controls in statistical models. Heckman and Hotz (1989) refer to this method of controlling as *selection on observables.* If observed variables capture all of the important differences, estimates of regression coefficients will be unbiased. However, if there are unobserved variables that affect both delinquency and dropout, then the classic problem of omitted variable bias will result, and the regression coefficients will be biased.

Since participation in delinquency and drug use cannot be randomly assigned, youth who vary in their degree of participation are also likely to differ on a wide array of individual characteristics, some of which may also cause dropping out. Some differences, such as a tendency toward youthful rebellion or an underlying "pseudomaturity" may be difficult to measure and control for in multiple regression analyses. The failure to take these differences into account may lead to misleading findings with regard to the effects of delinquency and drug use on dropping out.

The standard strategy for addressing these differences has been to control for observed selection factors in regression models. Table A-2 provides a summary of the various factors that have been controlled in the major studies that have been conducted on the effects of delinquency and drug use on dropout. Even researchers who have employed this strategy have expressed concern that some differences may not be adequately captured by variables available to them in the data set and have been cautionary about their findings. For example, Bachman et al. (1978) found that dropouts had higher rates of delinquency and substance use than graduates as far back as junior high school. However, they qualify their finding by noting: "Still another explanation is that the 'C causes both A and B' pattern of causation is heavily involved here: failure experiences in school lead to both delinquent behavior and (somewhat later when the young men reach or pass their sixteenth birthday) dropping out of school" (178).

Similarly, Friedman, Glickmand, and Utada (1983), who found that drug use was related to dropping out after controlling for 20 demographic, personal, and family variables associated with dropping out, caution, "It may be that the tendency of being dissatisfied with school and not enjoying school could be an underlying or more basic factor which predisposes to dropping out of high school as well as to become involved in drug use" (363). Indeed, when prior researchers have controlled for predictors of dropout, the association between delinquency and drug use and dropout is often substantially reduced or eliminated (Fagan and Pabon 1990; Krohn et al. 1995). Therefore, any study that seeks to assess the impact of delinquency and drug use on dropout must take seriously the possibility that selection rather than causation is driving the relationship between the three behaviors. This involves a strategy that facilitates making causal inferences about the effects of a "treatment" when only observational data are available.

THIS STUDY

This study provides a more rigorous test than prior research of the claim that delinquency and drug use are causes of dropping out by using econometric models for panel data. Panel data models, including random effects models and fixed effects models, which have not generally been applied to the study of dropout, can produce much better estimates of the effects of delinquency and drug use on dropping out than conventional regression models. Unlike conventional methods, which approximate randomization by relying on observed variables available to the researcher in the data set, these methods control for both observed and unobserved sources of heterogeneity. This is accomplished by relying on within-person variability to estimate the effects of covariates that are free from bias due to omitted individual characteristics that do not change over time, such an underlying tendency to engage in deviant behavior or a difficulty delaying gratification which might underlie a pseudomautiry. Such a strategy provides a substantial improvement over prior studies.

Second, this study takes into account the diversity of the dropout population and how this may be related to delinquency and drug use. As demonstrated by Janosz and LeBlanc (1998), not all dropouts are the same, and the effects of delinquency and drug use may differ depending on the type of dropout. Social class may be a particularly important difference between dropouts. Among middle-class dropouts, involvement in problem behaviors may be a stronger impetus to dropout, whereas lower-class dropouts may be more characterized by socioeconomic disadvantage and academic problems. Therefore, it is important to consider the effects of delinquency and drug use overall as well as for middle-class and lower-class dropouts separately. The distribution of different types of dropouts in prior studies may partially account for the divergent findings.

Third, research should also consider whether the reaction to delinquency and drug use determines whether they lead to dropping out. Delinquency and drug use are behaviors that, if detected, may result in sanctions, such as being suspended from school or arrested by police. Delinquency and drug use may not lead to dropout if they go undetected or unpunished. Fourth, when possible, research should also utilize nationally representative data. With the exception of Mensch and Kandel's (1988) event history analysis of the NLSY79 cohort data, studies on this topic have generally employed localized samples that are small and non-representative. Samples that are not nationally representative are likely to produce findings that are not generalizable. Moreover, this is especially problematic given the strong likelihood that delinquency and drug use may play different roles in the etiology of dropout for youth from different social classes. Samples that are not representative could bias the findings in the direction of whatever associations and effects are characteristic of one or another type of dropout.

CHAPTER 3

Distinguishing Causes from Symptoms

THE NLSY97

This study uses data from the National Longitudinal Survey of Youth 1997 (NLSY97), sponsored by the U.S. Bureau of Labor Statistics. The NLSY97 is a nationally representative longitudinal survey of youth who were 12 to 16 years old on the sampling date of December 31, 1996 (or who were born between 1980 and 1984). The NLSY97 is designed to document the transition from school to work and into adulthood. The NLSY97 sample is composed of two independent probability samples: (1) a cross-sectional sample of 6,748 youths who are representative of the noninstitutionalized population of youths in the U.S. who were born between 1980 and 1984, and (2) an oversample of 2,236 black and Hispanic youths. The cohort was selected this way to meet the survey design requirement of providing enough black and Hispanic respondents for statistical analyses.

The NLSY97 cohort was selected in two phases. In the first phase, a list of housing units was derived from a stratified multistage area probability sample. The list of eligible housing units was composed of 96,512 households. In the second phase, subsamples of eligible persons identified in the first phase were selected. Screener interviews were completed in 75,291 households to identify individuals in the appropriate age range for the study. Of the 9,806 respondents who were identified as eligible for the survey, 8,984 participated in round 1 of the survey, which took place in 1997 (91.6 percent of eligible respondents).[2] Follow-up interviews with the original respondents are conducted annually. Nine waves of data (or through 2005) are currently available. NLS surveys are known for their relatively high sample retention rates. In the case of the NLSY97, 81.7 percent or 7,338 of the original round 1 respondents also participated in round 9 (2005). In addition to annual youth interviews, data were collected from the responding parent in round 1, school surveys in 1996 and 2000, and transcripts when respondents left high school or turned age 18 if they were still enrolled. Transcript data are available for 6,232 youth (69.4 percent). Data from the youth interview and parent interview are used in this study.

VARIABLES

Dropout

A full list of variable definitions is provided in Table A-3. The dependent variable in this study is dropout. Determining who is a dropout is the most critical yet difficult task in any study on dropout. The measure of dropout used in this study is derived from self-reports of school enrollment at each round of the NLSY97. Respondents are asked a series of questions at each interview to determine their school enrollment status. School enrollment status at the previous round is confirmed and corrected at each round.[3] NLSY97 staff created a variable that summarizes the youth's enrollment status at each round based on the information collected on school enrollment. Using this variable, a dropout is defined as anyone who is not currently enrolled in school and who does not have a high school diploma. Following the conventions in the dropout literature, GED holders are counted as dropouts. However, since several studies have indicated a strong association between delinquency and drug use and getting a GED (Chuang 1997; Mensch and Kandel 1988; Obot and Anthony 2000), a second measure of dropout is constructed that counts GED holders as high school graduates to test the sensitivity of the findings to the definition of dropout.

The measure of dropout used in this study is likely to be a conservative one since several types of youth are not counted as dropouts. First, youth who dropped out temporarily before round 1 and who returned to school by round 1 are not counted as dropouts since they were enrolled in school at round 1. Second, youth who dropped out temporarily between interviews and who reenrolled in school by their next interview are also not counted as dropouts. While the NLSY97 does query youth on gaps of one month or more in enrollment between interviews and before round 1 (in the parent interview), making it possible to count such youth as dropouts, this information is not used here because information on delinquency and drug use is only available on an annual rather than monthly basis and is not available prior to round 1. This study is primarily interested in whether delinquent behavior and drug use in one year predicts dropping out in the next year. The use of dropout status on the interview date rather than any time away from school is less likely to capture truants and more likely to capture more actual dropouts.

Quality of Data on Dropout

Despite the recent debate over the dropout rate, the quality of data on dropout in studies at the individual level is often given short shrift in the methods sections of papers. This may have to do with the fact that researchers using secondary data sets often have little control over the quality of the data that is available to them. However, I believe that there are two major strengths of the NLSY97 for studying dropout. First, unlike most prior studies that have examined this issue, which are limited by the fact that dropout is measured for only one wave in the study, the NLSY97 contains information on dropout measured at every wave of the survey, which allows more precise measurement of the timing of dropout. Moreover, this strategy captures dropouts who subsequently return to school. As Finn (1991) notes, "dropping out is not the simplistic 'now I'm here – now I'm not' phenomenon assumed (by default) in studies that compare those who graduate with those who do not" (29). These types of returning dropouts are often not distinguished in studies of dropout.

A second strength of the NLSY97 is that it likely does a better job of keeping dropouts in the sample than other national data sets. Dropouts are difficult to follow and are likely to be underrepresented in most studies. The NLSY97 is less likely to suffer from this problem because the attrition rate in the NLSY97 is quite low. Prominent prior studies on the effects of delinquency and drug use on dropout have suffered from sample attrition problems (for example, see Kaplan and Liu 1994). Over 90 percent of respondents in the NLSY97 have more than one interview (Olson 2005; Pierret et al. 2007). Second, the NLSY97 utilizes a household rather than a school-based sample. In a school-based sample, youth who dropped out of school early would not be in school and would therefore not be eligible to be sampled in the first place. This problem would be less serious in a household-based sample.

The NLSY97 is not without its limitations for studying dropout, however. First, while better than a school-based survey, as a household-based survey the NLSY97 might still have difficulty identifying respondents for initial participation if they were not attached to a household in round 1. For example, youth who were homeless or incarcerated would not have been included in the sample. Since these youth are especially likely not to be in school, this could be problematic. However, this problem is likely to be less of a problem than in a school-based survey, which is typically used to study dropout.

Second, the measure of dropping out used in this study is primarily based on youth self-reports. There are reasons to believe that this source of information may not be entirely reliable. For reasons having to do with social desirability, youth may misrepresent their school enrollment. If a youth misrepresents his or her current enrollment status, then the information would be misleading and have the effect of underestimating the true extent of dropout.

Delinquency and Drug Use

Although the main focus of the NLSY97 is on the educational and labor market experiences of youth, the data set collects information on a wide range of topics, including respondents' involvement in delinquency, criminal behavior, and substance use. Information on delinquency and substance use is collected as part of the *self-administered* portion of the Youth Questionnaire (Self-Administered Questionnaire, or SAQ). In addition to delinquency and substance use, the SAQ collected information on other sensitive topics, including relationships with parents, dating, and sexual activity. During this part of the interview, the respondent uses an audio computer-assisted self-interview (ACASI). The youth has the option of listening to the questions with earphones or turning off the audio and reading the questions from the computer screen. ACASI interviews were conducted in either English or Spanish.

The Office of Juvenile Justice and Delinquency Prevention of the U.S. Department of Justice sponsors a series of questions in SAQ of the NLSY97 that focuses on respondents' involvement in delinquent and criminal behavior (CHRR 2003). The NLSY97 delinquency items are modified versions of items developed by Del Elliott to measure delinquency and criminality in the National Youth Survey (NYS) (CHRR 2003: Appendix 9). However, the range of delinquent offenses on which respondents were queried in the NLSY97 is not as wide as in the NYS and should be thought of as representing a more serious subset of possible offenses. The SAQ also collects information on respondents' use of licit and illicit substances. These questions were modified from questions in the National Survey of Family and Households (NSFH-2) (CHRR 2003: Appendix 9)

Most studies on delinquency and drug use are interested in the causes of such behavior. This study, in contrast, focuses on the consequences of delinquency and drug use. That is, deviant behavior is treated as an independent rather than the dependent variable. However, the same considerations that go into measuring delinquency and drug use outcomes also apply when offending is the key independent variable of interest. Self-report measures of delinquency, such as those available in the NLSY97, are the most ubiquitous in studies of offending, as data on arrests tends to drastically underestimate the true extent of delinquency. However, what is not agreed upon is how exactly to combine multiple delinquency items into a single scale. The measure employed most often is a frequency scale, which sums the number of times a respondent committed each offense, usually within some limited period of time, such as the previous 6 months or year. Unfortunately, frequency scales are prone to many problems. Osgood, McMorris, and Potenza (2002) outline three weaknesses of frequency scales. First, since most delinquent offenses are rare, frequency scales tend to have distributions that are heavily skewed toward zero. This heavy skewness allows a relatively small number of cases to be highly (disproportionately) influential in the estimation of slopes or intercepts in a regression analysis. Second, frequency scales assume equal intervals, such that the difference between 0 and 1 offenses is the same as the difference between, say, 10 and 11 offenses. If this were the case, interpretation of the effects of delinquency would not be the same at levels of delinquency. Third, because minor offenses occur more frequently than serious offenses, frequency scales place undue weight on more minor delinquency. Individuals with a high score on a frequency scale may have committed a trivial offense many times but never have committed a serious offense.

A good alternative to a frequency scale is what is referred to as a variety scale of antisocial involvement. Hindelang, Hirschi, and Weis (1981) found that an "ever variety" measure was superior to a measure of frequency in the past year. This measure counts the number of different types of delinquent behaviors in which a respondent has ever participated (hence the term variety). Summative variety measures resolve some of the problems of frequency scales. First, they reduce the skewness of the distribution. Second, they do not suffer from the problem of unequal intervals since they focus only on the "ever-never" distinction. Third, more minor offenses are not over counted since a youth would have to commit both minor and serious offenses in order to score high on the variety scale. Variety scales have been found to have higher levels of internal consistency, more reliability over time, and stronger associations with conceptually relevant variables (Bendixen, Endresen, and Olweus 2003).

This study employs variety measures of both delinquency and drug use. The measure of delinquency taps respondents' participation in 21 criminal offenses since the last interview: (1) carrying a handgun, (2) vandalism, (3) petty theft, (4) petty shoplifting, (5) petty larceny, (6) petty burglary, (7) petty armed robbery, (8) major theft, (9) major shoplifting, (10) major larceny, (11) major burglary, (12) major armed robbery, (13) grand theft auto, (14) receiving income from stolen property, (15) other property crimes (including possessing or receiving stolen property), (16) income from other property crimes, (17) aggravated assault, (18) selling illegal drugs, (19) selling marijuana, (20) selling hard drugs, and (21) income from selling drugs. The delinquency variety scale therefore ranges from 0 to 21, with higher values indicating greater participation in delinquency. The delinquency variety scale does not overweight more minor offenses, since the only way to get a high score on the scale is to commit both serious and minor offenses. One caveat for the variety scale is that in 1997, for some offenses, respondents were queried on whether they ever participated in the behavior rather than whether they participated in the past year.[4] Therefore, the measure of variety in 1997 refers to having ever committed the offense by round 1 rather than to having committed it in the past year. To address this issue in the statistical models, the number of months since the last interview (or since birth) is controlled so that all youth are on equal footing with regard to the time period for possibly committing delinquency.

In terms of drug use, youth are asked annually about their use of the following three substances: (1) tobacco, (2) alcohol, and (3) marijuana.[5] For each substance, youth are asked whether they ever used it, how old they were when they first used, and how many times they used it in the past month. Additional information is elicited for specific substances. For cigarettes, information is collected on the number of cigarettes smoked per day in the last 30 days. For alcohol, information on the quantity is solicited, and for alcohol and marijuana, frequency of use before or during school or work is obtained. The measure of drug use employed here counts the variety of participation in seven different drug use activities in the month preceding the survey: (1) smoking cigarettes, (2) smoking more than one pack of cigarettes per day (defined as more than 20 cigarettes per day), (3) drinking alcohol, (4) drinking alcohol before or during school or work, (5) binge drinking (defined as having 5 or more drinks on one occasion), (6) using marijuana, and (7) using marijuana before or during school or work. The variety scale for drug use therefore ranges from 0 to 7, with higher scores indicating greater participation in drug use. The use of a past month (as opposed to past year) variety measure likely means that more severe users are being captured, since youth who used in the past month rather than at all in the past year are more likely to be chronic users.[6] I do not present alpha reliabilities for the delinquency and drug use variety measures because they are indices, not scales. That is, I do not expect that involvement in one type of delinquency (or use of one type of substance) will necessarily be correlated with another. Table A-4 provides descriptions of the specific items used in the construction of the delinquency and drug use scales.

<u>Quality of Data on Delinquency and Drug Use</u>
As was the case when measuring dropout, it is important to consider the strengths and limitations of self-reported data on delinquency and drug use. The first issue that needs to be considered is the possibility that delinquency and drug use may be underreported, given that such behavior is considered deviant and could result in punishment. With the exception of the written permission forms that had to be signed by youths' parents, the entire NLSY97 survey was conducted using computer-assisted personal interviewing (CAPI) (Michael and Pergamit 2001). As previous mentioned, items querying respondents on sensitive topics were administered as part of the self-administered questionnaire (SAQ). In the SAQ, respondents read questions on a computer screen while simultaneously listening to them being played in earphones. They entered their response directly into the computer by pressing a key. This type of interviewing technique has several benefits over traditional paper-and-pencil (PAPI) interviewing

(Thornberry and Krohn 2000). First, it overcomes reading problems. Second, it prevents youth from having to reveal potentially embarrassing information directly to another person. Since most interviews were conducted at home, it also prevents parents from hearing the answers (Michael and Pergamit 2001). The use of the SAQ for delinquency and drug use decreased interviewer error and increased response rates to sensitive questions (Zagorsky and Gardecki 1998). There is some evidence, however, that when interviews were conducted by telephone, in which case SAQ was not available, respondents were less willing to report these behaviors (Wang and Krishnamurty 2008). Telephone interviews were conducted with between 3 and 16 percent of respondents, depending on the round (CHRR 2005).

However, questionnaire administration might not be the only reason why underreporting might occur. Another reason has to do with the fact that the NLSY97 relies on a household sample. Although household samples likely do a much better job of including serious offenders and drug users than school samples, it is still possible that serious juvenile offenders and drug addicts are underrepresented in the sample. This is because a household sample would have difficulty catching serious offenders who do not live at home (they may be incarcerated or live on the streets) or who do not spend a lot of time at home. The NLSY97 is a sample of non-institutionalized U.S. youth.

One final issue that deserves mention is the relationship between self-reported delinquency and race. Some studies suggest that minority youth, particularly black males, are likely to underreport their involvement in delinquency in surveys (Kim, Fendrich, and Wislar 2000; Maxfield, Weiler, and Widom 2000; Piquero, Macintosh, and Hickman 2002). However, there is some evidence that the use of modern interviewing techniques, such the SAQ employed in the NLSY97, may yield more accurate self-reports of delinquency among minority youth (Paschall, Ornstein, and Flewelling 2001). However, other researchers (Bushway et al. 2000) that have used the NLSY97 to examine delinquency and crime have found that minority youth report less delinquency than white youth, suggesting that the NLSY97 may still suffer from problems of underreporting of delinquency by minority youth. Since black and Hispanic youth are likely to overrepresented in the poverty sample, it is important to examine differences in the effects of delinquency and drug use by race within social class to be sure that any lesser effects among poor youth are not due to underreporting among minorities.

Social Class

In studies on dropout, social class is usually tapped using a traditional measure of SES, which is a composite of parental income, parental education, and parental occupational status. The measure of social class used as a moderating variable in this study is a measure of poverty status (measures of parental education and household income are used as controls variables, as will be discussed later). Poverty status was constructed using the ratio of the youth's household income to the poverty line in 1996 calendar year. This measure was constructed by NLS staff using information on the federal poverty threshold in 1996, the size of the family, and the number of children under age 18. Youth who are at or below the poverty line are coded 1 on this measure. Youth who are above the poverty line are coded 0. A continuous measure of social class is not used because this study is concerned with differences between lower and higher classes. The theory specifies that delinquency and drug use operate differently youth from different social classes. A continuous measure of SES would bias the results away from finding a significant interaction of delinquency and drug use with social class. A measure of poverty status captures the major differences between different social classes, such as persistent unemployment and poverty (Jarjoura 1996).[7]

Social Sanctions

In order to examine whether delinquency and drug use effects depend on whether a youth is sanctioned for the behavior, this study employs two measures of sanctions: school suspension and arrest. These actions represent responses by others to the youth's behavior. The schooling section of the NLSY97 queries respondents who had been in enrolled in an elementary or secondary school since the last interview on whether they had ever been suspended from school, how many days they had been suspended, and in what grades they had been suspended. Using this information, I constructed a dichotomous variable coded 1 if a youth was suspended from school for at least one day since the last interview and 0 if they had not been suspended. At each wave, respondents are also asked about their involvement with the criminal justice system. Using this sinformation, I constructed a dichotomous variable coded 1 if a youth had been arrested since the last interview and 0 if not.[8]

Control Variables

Dropping out is not randomly assigned; rather, youth are self-selected into dropping out based on their socioeconomic, family, academic, and psychological backgrounds. The characteristics of youth that predict dropping out are also likely to predict participation in delinquency and drug use. Although the main contribution of this study is the use of panel data models to control for selection on *unobserved* differences, I adjust for as many background variables as possible that prior research has shown are related to dropout, delinquency, and drug use. The relative contribution of unobserved selection factors can be compared to models that just control for selection measures in the data set. Moreover, it is especially important to control for time-varying covariates, such as changes in family structure or academic performance, since the models employed do not address this type of selection but rather only selection on stable individual differences. Because I have hypothesized that there might be unobserved selection factors not available in the data set, however, I assume that, consistent with prior research, including these observed variables will not account for all of the differences between youth relevant to delinquency, drug use, and dropout. Specifically, since I assume that these unmeasured difference drive youth to engage in delinquency, drug use, and dropout, I expect that observed controls might reduce, but not eliminate, the effects of delinquency and drug use on dropout.

Controls can be grouped into several broad categories. The first group of control variables address differences in demographic background characteristics. *Gender* is controlled by including a dummy variable coded 1 for males and 0 for females. *Race and ethnicity* is controlled with a series of dummy variables for black, Hispanic, Asian, and other races, with white as the reference category. *Age* is a time-varying covariate indicating the youth's age in years at each interview. The NLSY97 does not contain information on parents' occupation that would allow me to create a standard measure of youths' socioeconomic status. However, I was able to include information on *household income* from 1996 as well as *parental education*, which is the maximum number of years of schooling completed by either residential parent (mother or father) by 1997.[9,10] (The statistical models employed will control for stable unmeasured differences in SES, however). A variable is also included that indicates each respondent's *mother's age when she gave birth* to the respondent, measured in years.

A time-varying dummy variable is also included for *urbanicity* at each wave (with rural as the reference category). A time-varying control for region of residence and a time-invariant control for birth cohort are also controlled.

Because family experiences are strongly related to delinquency, drug use, and dropout, various aspects of the youth's family were measured and included as control variables. *Family structure* was measured using a series of time-varying dummy variables for single mother, single father, stepparent, and other parent figure, using both biological parents as the reference category. *Mother supportive* is measured in 1997 only and indicates on a scale of 1 to 3 (1=not very supportive, 2=somewhat supportive, 3=very supportive) how supportive the respondent believes his or her primary mother figure is. *Mother permissive* is a dummy variable coded 1 if a youth rated his mother's discipline as permissive and 0 if he rated it as not permissive. This variable was also only measured in 1997. Finally, a variable indicating the total *number of different residences* a youth has lived at since age 12 is also included as a measure of residential mobility, which is updated at each round.

Because school experiences are likely to predispose youth to both deviant behavior and dropping out, it is important to control for measures of school performance and engagement. *Academic performance* is measured using self-reports of the respondents' grades in middle school on an eight-point scale (1=mostly below Ds, 2=mostly Ds, 3=half Ds/halfCs, 4=mostly Cs, 5=half Cs/half Bs, 6=mostly Bs, 7=half Bs/half As, 8=mostly As). Because *grade retention* is strongly linked to dropout and delinquency, a self-reported measure is included that indicates whether a respondent has ever repeated a grade by each round. Summary percentile score for four key subjects (Mathematical Knowledge, Arithmetic Reasoning, Word Knowledge, and Paragraph Comprehension) on the computer-adaptive form of the *Armed Services Vocational Aptitude Battery* (CAT-ASVAB), which was administered to most respondents at Round 1, is also included. A time-varying measure of the number of schools a youth attended since 7th grade is also included, since changing schools is predictive of dropout (Rumberger 1995; Swanson and Schneider 1999). While correlated with the residential mobility measure, this measure is not so highly correlated as to create problems with multicolinearity, as many youth move or change schools without experiencing the other (Swanson and Schneider 1999). A youth's *attachment to school* is measured with a summative scale of 5 items measured in round 1 only that indicate how much the youth agrees with statements such as "teachers are interested in students" or "grading is fair." Finally, a measure of youth's *exposure to deviant peer influence*, also only measured in round 1, is also included. Insofar as variables which are truly time-varying are treated as time-invariant, coefficient estimates will be biased.

I also control for involvement in adult roles that might lead to dropping out or that represent an underlying tendency toward youthful rebellion. Since the NLSY97 was designed to study the labor market experiences of youth, it contains particularly rich information on employment. In particular, it contains weekly employment diaries indicating the respondents' employment status and hours worked for each week since age 14. Using this information, I first calculated the total number of hours worked in the calendar year prior to each interview. Second, I calculated the number of weeks a respondent worked for that year. I then divided the total number of hours worked by the number of weeks worked to get the average number of hours worked when working throughout the year. I then created a dummy variable for intensive employment indicating whether a youth worked more than an average of 20 hours per week in the calendar year preceding the interview. The threshold of 20 hours per week was used to be consistent with prior studies on the effects of employment on dropout (Staff and Lee 2007), which shows that high intensity employment specifically is associated with dropout.

A second adult role is involvement in sexual relationships. First, a time-varying dummy variable was constructed indicating whether a youth has ever had *sexual intercourse.* Second, I constructed two dummy variables indicating whether a youth's relationships status. The first indicated whether the youth had ever married by each year. The second variable indicates whether the respondent was living with an opposite sex partner at each survey date. These two variables are exclusive. That is, marriage takes precedence over living with a sexual partner. Youth who were ever married cannot be coded as living with a sexual partner at the interview date. Only youth who have never been married can be coded as such. Both variables are included in the regression models together. A final time-varying dummy variable indicates whether a youth has *ever had a child.*

Finally, I control for *exposure time.* Exposure time is the number of months elapsed between each interview. This is necessary because there is considerable variability in the interview schedule from round to round, and youth with longer periods of time elapsed would have more time to drop out and more time to commit delinquency and engage in drug use. In round 1 delinquency models, exposure time refers to the number of months elapsed since birth. This is because the round 1 measure of delinquency refers to having ever committed the offenses.

Sample

Not all of the 8,984 youth who participated in round 1 of the NLSY97 are included in this study. Table A-5 describes the restrictions made to obtain the final NLSY97 sample and the number and percentage of respondents lost due to each restriction. I made several restrictions that reduced the sample to 6,211 youth. To do this, I first arranged the data from rounds 1 through 7 into a person-year format, where the unit of analysis was a youth in a particular survey year. I then deleted any person-year that had missing data on the dropout, delinquency, or drug use measures. I applied two additional restrictions to arrive at the final sample. First, I deleted all of the observations for a youth if he or she did not have at least three waves of data available. I did this because the random effects models I used require at least three records per individual when a lagged independent variable is used. Second, I also deleted youth with missing data on the poverty status variable.

In the final sample, each of the 6,211 youth contributes between three and seven survey years of data to the analysis, meaning that the panel is unbalanced. Because lagged measures of delinquency and drug use are used, each youth contributes between two and six person-year observations to the data set. Table A-6 reports the number of person-year observations contributed by each youth in the sample. As can be seen, most youth contribute all 6 person-year observations. Over 70 percent of youth contribute six person-years to the data set.

The fact that 30 percent of the sample is not included raises concern about sample selection bias. If exclusion from the sample is not random, the estimates of the coefficients could be biased. To evaluate this, I examined differences in all of the variables used in the analysis measured at round 1 between youth who were excluded and youth who were included in the sample. Table A-8 presents the results of this analysis.

As shown in Table A-8, youth who are not included in the sample are no more likely than youth who are included to have already been dropouts at round 1 or to be more involved in drug use in the month before the round 1 interview. However, youth who are not included in the study reported *less* involvement in delinquency in the year before round 1 than did youth who were included. While it may be surprising that youth who are not included are less involved in delinquency, this finding may reflect the possibility that minority youth—who, as shown in the table, are less likely to be included in the sample—are underreporting their involvement in delinquency. Several studies have found that minority youth, particularly black males, tend to underreport their involvement in delinquency (Piquero et al. 2002). There is some evidence that this is also a problem in the NLSY97 (Bushway et al. 2000).

There are some other differences between the two groups in the control variables. Youth who were not included were slightly older at round 1. Youth who are included are more likely to have parents who are high school dropouts and less likely to have parents who went to college. Non-included youth are also more likely to come from urban settings but less likely to have mothers who are permissive. They also have lower standardized test scores and more exposure to antisocial peer influence. There are no differences in terms of adult roles or behaviors, however. There are some regional differences, though, with youth in the Northeast being underrepresented in the included sample and youth in the Midwest being somewhat overrepresented.

While it is important that there are no differences in dropout status at round 1 between the samples, the systematic differences uncovered do raise concerns. To address sample selection due to attrition, the NLS staff provide panel weights that adjust for differential attrition on the basis of gender, race, and age at the round 1 interview. However, these weights do not address sample selection bias due to having deleted youth with missing data on delinquency, drug use, or poverty status. It is likely that the differential sample selection reported here, to the extent that it exists, has the effect of biasing the results in a conservative direction.

Table A-7 presents descriptive statistics for the final sample for all variables used in the analysis. Descriptive statistics are pooled across survey waves and presented for all youth and for poor and not poor youth separately. Among the entire sample, youth report being a dropout in about 13 percent of the person-years. Dropout is much more prevalent among poor youth, however, who report being dropouts in 27 percent of the person-years relative to only 10 percent of the person-years for non-poor youth. Delinquency variety is also higher among poor youth, but drug use is higher among non-poor youth. Being suspended from school and arrested are relatively uncommon, with 8 percent of the person-years reporting suspension and 5 percent reporting arrest. Both school suspension and arrest are more common among poor youth. More detailed descriptive analyses, especially for delinquency and drug use, will be presented in the next chapter.

Missing Data

Missing data on all of the independent variables other than delinquency and drug use, including both time-invariant and time-varying covariates, were imputed using multiple imputation (Allison 2002). Multiple imputation improves on conventional imputation methods by deliberately introducing random variation into the imputation process. However, the handling of missing data is complicated by the longitudinal nature of the data. Because software for performing multiple imputation with panel data or clustered data is not readily available and difficult to use, I used a method that takes into account the dependence among the multiple observations for each individual. While the data were still formatted so that there was only one record per individual, with distinct variables for measurements at different ages, I used all of the variables in the model as predictors to impute missing data on the other variables. In this way, an individual's value at one point in time is used to impute missing data for that individual at a later point in time. The dependent variable—dropout—was used in the imputation process, although as I mentioned above, I did not impute this variable. Each missing value was imputed with five plausible values, producing five imputed data sets. These five data sets were then used to estimate the model five times—one for each imputed data set—and were combined to produce the results. This involved averaging the coefficients and correcting the standard errors to account for the random variation introduced into the imputed values.

Due to the complex nature of the NLSY97 sampling design, the data must be weighted and standard errors corrected for design effects before drawing inferences from the data. Since the NLSY97 actually consists of two samples—a cross-sectional sample that is representative of non-institutionalized U.S. youth and an oversample of black and Hispanic youth, weighting the data is necessary in order to produce estimates that are generalizable to the population. I do this for all descriptive analyses. However, following the advice of the NLS staff, regression analyses are not weighted but rather indicator variables are included for primary selection factors (e.g., race).[11]

Econometric Models for Panel Data

<u>Do Delinquency and Drug Use Lead to Dropout, or are Delinquency and Drug Use Caused by the Same Factors that Cause Dropout?</u>
One of the main contributions of this study is to determine whether prior delinquency and prior drug use lead to dropping out or whether all three of the behaviors are effects of a common cause. Because delinquency, drug use, and dropping out are likely caused by many of the same factors, such as socioeconomic disadvantage, an early state of disengagement from school, or an underlying tendency to engage in deviant behavior, any observed relationships among delinquency, drug use, and dropping out may be spurious rather than reflecting the causal effect of delinquency or drug use on dropping out. As mentioned earlier, prior studies that have examined this issue have relied on observational data and are generally unable to make causal inferences because the individuals observed were not randomly assigned to "treatment" and "control" conditions. Because different levels of delinquency and drug use cannot be randomly assigned, differences in delinquency and drug use are also correlated with differences in factors that predict dropout. Some of these important differences may be captured by including observed covariates in multiple regression models, whereas other differences—such as early school disengagement or an underlying tendency toward youthful deviance—may be difficult or impossible to measure. If these variables are omitted from the model and are correlated with delinquency or drug use, then the coefficient estimates for the effects of delinquency and drug use will be biased. Specifically, it is hypothesized that the coefficients for delinquency and drug use will be biased in the direction of overstating their influence on dropping out.

Concerns over this type of omitted variable bias have led researchers to adopt random and fixed effects models for panel data. Random effects models and fixed effects models control for unobserved heterogeneity in slightly different ways. Random effects models make more restrictive assumptions than fixed effects models. In particular, they assume that the error term is normally distributed, making them more efficient to estimate than fixed effects models because one only has to estimate the standard deviation of the distribution. The random effects model also assumes that the right-hand-side variables are uncorrelated with the omitted variables for which one is trying to control, an assumption that is highly problematic in the case of delinquency, drug use, and dropout. This assumption means that the random effects model does not control for all stable individual differences. Because the random effects model relies on both between-person and within-person variation to estimate the coefficients, however, it does allow for the estimation of the effects of time-variant covariates.

Fixed effects models relax some of the assumptions of random effects models. In particular, they make no parametric assumptions about the distribution of the unobserved heterogeneity, and individual-specific effects are allowed to be correlated with observed variables. For this reason, fixed effects models control for all unmeasured characteristics of individuals that are stable over time. Since fixed effects models rely only on the within-individual variation to estimate the coefficients, coefficients for variables that do not change over time (e.g. gender or race) cannot be estimated, although it is possible to estimate models that include interactions with time-invariant covariates. A more technical discussion of these models can be found in Hsiao (2003) and Greene (2003).

This study uses a "hybrid" random effects method that combines the advantages of both fixed and random effects (Allison 2005). The basic random effects model can be written as follows:

$$y_{it} = \alpha_i + \gamma' Z_i + \beta'_1 X_{it-1} + \beta'_2 D_{it-1} + u_{it} \qquad \text{(eq. 1)}$$

where α_i is the intercept, Z_i is a vector of time-invariant characteristics associated with each individual (e.g., gender, race), X_{it-1} is a vector of time-varying individual characteristics (e.g., age) all measured at the previous round, D_{it-1} is delinquency or drug use variety measured at the previous wave, and u_{it} is the error term. The error term can be decomposed into two parts:

$$u_{it} = \tau_i + \varepsilon_{it} \qquad \text{(eq. 2)}$$

where τ_i represents the individual-specific time-stable individual differences and ε_{it} represents individual- and time-varying random error term. The time invariant error term, τ_i, is assumed to follow a normal distribution. The random error term, ε_{it}, is assumed to be uncorrelated with the predictors Z_i, X_{it-1}, and τ_i.

This last assumption of the random effects model is problematic, since it means that the model does not control for unmeasured stable individual differences. The approach is to decompose the time-varying independent variables in the random effects model into two parts: one representing the between-person variation and one representing the within-person variation. The between-person component is simply the mean of the variable for each individual across time points or group mean and is expressed as follows:

$$\overline{X} = \frac{1}{T} \cdot \sum_{i=1}^{T} X_{it} \qquad\qquad \text{(eq. 3)}$$

The within-person component is the difference between each individual's group mean and his or her variable value at each time point:

$$\Delta X_{it} = X_{it} - \overline{X}_i \qquad\qquad \text{(eq. 4)}$$

These decomposed variables are then used as predictors in a random effects model. The hybrid model can be written as follows:

$$y_{it} = \alpha_i + \gamma' Z_i + \beta'_{b_1 i} \overline{X}_i + \beta'_{w_1 i} \Delta X_{it} + \beta'_{b_2 i} \overline{D}_i + \beta'_{w_2 i} \Delta D_{it} + u_{it} \quad \text{(eq. 5)}$$

This approach has several advantages. First, it provides coefficient estimates for the between-person effects as well as for any measured time-invariant variables. Second, the decomposition ensures that the within-individual estimates are uncorrelated with the time-constant part of the error term, and the coefficient should be a consistent estimate of the within-individual relationship between prior delinquency and drug use and later dropping out. In other words, the within-individual estimates should be the same as those obtained in a classic fixed effects model.   The fixed effects method is no panacea, however, since it cannot control for the effects of unmeasured variables that change over time. Nevertheless, it does address an important potential source of selection that is consistent with existing alternative explanations for delinquency, drug use, and dropout and that has not been addressed by prior studies.

My main focus here is on the within-person coefficients for prior delinquency and prior drug use. The between-person coefficients for time-varying covariates are confounded by average between-person differences in the outcomes. That is, they show us how youth who differ in terms of delinquency and drug use participation also differ across all years in terms of their dropout risk. Mean differences in dropout between youth do not lend themselves to causal interpretation, since they may be attributable to preexisting differences rather than to delinquency or drug use. A positive and statistically significant between-person coefficient for delinquency or drug can be interpreted to mean that youth with higher levels of delinquency or drug use across the observation period are more likely to be dropouts than are youth with lower levels of involvement. The within-individual coefficients for delinquency and drug use, on the other hand, shows how changes in delinquency or drug use are associated with changes in dropout status. Because they rely only on the within-individual change, they cannot be confounded by preexisting differences. That is, any change in dropout status that follows a change in delinquency or drug use cannot be due to preexisting, time-stable individual differences. The within-person coefficients therefore approximate the causal effect of delinquency and drug use on dropout. A positive and significant within-person coefficient tells us that delinquency or drug use leads to changes in dropout status, whereas a coefficient that is not significantly different from 0 indicates that delinquency (or drug use) and dropping out are spuriously related. Between-person effects can be calculated for all covariates, but within-person effects can only be calculated for time-varying covariates. My main focus here is on the within-individual coefficients. For examples of this method used in the literature, see Paternoster et al. (2003) and Gasper, DeLuca, and Estacion (2010).

I model the effects of delinquency and drug use on dropout using logistic regression models. In an effort to ensure proper causal ordering, I lagged all of the independent variables, including delinquency and drug use, by one year. Variables measured in 1997 (e.g., sex, race, socioeconomic status) are included as non-time varying controls only. If any of these variables are actually time-varying, coefficient estimates would be biased. Three different nested models were run for delinquency and drug use separately. First, a series of stepwise models was run which included only delinquency or drug use as a predictor to get "upper bound" estimates of the effects of delinquency and drug use on dropout. A second series of models was run which includes delinquency or drug use plus all of the control variables. Finally, a third set of models included random effects and unobserved controls for between-person differences.

Are the effects of delinquency and drug use different for youth from different social classes?

In order to address this question, I included interactions between delinquency and poverty status and drug use and poverty status in the statistical models. Interactions were included in all three nested models mentioned earlier. In the random effects model, both the between-person and within-person components for delinquency and drug use were interacted with the measure of arrest. Interacting the between-person component is necessary to control for any interaction at the between-person level. But the main interest is in interpreting the within-person interaction term, since that gives the effect of changes in the interaction on changes in dropout. The random effects model can be written:

$$y_{it} = \alpha_i + \gamma' Z_i + \beta'_{b_1 i} \overline{X}_i + \beta'_{w_1 i} \Delta X_{it} + \beta'_{b_2 i} \overline{D}_i + \beta'_{w_2 i} \Delta D_{it} + \beta'_{b_3 i} P_i +$$
$$\beta'_{b_4 i} \overline{D}_i * P_i + \beta'_{w_4 i} \Delta D_{it} * \Delta P_i + u_{it}$$

(eq. 6)

Since an interaction between the within-person term for delinquency (or drug use) and poverty is included in the model, the "main effect" term of delinquency gives the effect of changes in delinquency participation in changes in dropout status when poverty status is equal to 0. In other words, it gives the effect of delinquency or drug use for non-poor youth. To get the effect for poor youth, one must combine the interaction term with the main effect for delinquency. A negative and significant interaction term would indicate that delinquency has a smaller effect on dropout for poor youth.

Do the Effects of Delinquency and Drug Use on Dropout Depend on What Happens to Youth as a Result of Delinquency and Drug Use?

In order to address this question, I included interactions between delinquency and drug use and suspension and arrest in the random effects model. Both the between-person and within-person components for delinquency and drug use were interacted with the measure of arrest. Interacting the between-person component is necessary to control for any interaction at the between-person level. But the main interest is in interpreting the within-person interaction term. The random effects model can be written:

$$y_{it} = \alpha_i + \gamma' Z_i + \beta'_{b_1 i} \overline{X}_i + \beta'_{w_1 i} \Delta X_{it} + \beta'_{b_2 i} \overline{D}_i + \beta'_{w_2 i} \Delta D_{it} +$$

$$\beta'_{b_3 i} \overline{S}_i + \beta' \Delta S_{w_3 i} + \beta'_{b_4 i} \overline{D}_i * \overline{S}_i + \beta'_{w_4 i} \Delta D_{it} * \Delta S_i + u_{it}$$

(eq. 7)

Since an interaction between the within-person term for delinquency (or drug use) and arrest is included in the model, the "main effect" term of delinquency gives the effect of changes in delinquency participation in changes in dropout status for youth who were not arrested. To get the effect for youth who were arrested, one must combine the interaction term with the main effect for delinquency and arrest. A positive and significant interaction term would indicate that being arrested increases the effects of delinquency or drug use on dropout.

<u>Are the conditioning effects of social sanctions on delinquency and drug use different for youth from different social classes?</u>
In order to address this question, I included three-way interactions between delinquency and suspension and poverty status in the random effects model. The random effects model can be written:

$$y_{it} = \alpha_i + \gamma' Z_i + \beta'_{b_1 i} \overline{X}_i + \beta'_{w_1 i} \Delta X_{it} +$$

$$\beta'_{b_2 i} \overline{D}_i + \beta'_{w_2 i} \Delta D_{it} +$$

$$\beta'_{b_3 i} \overline{S}_i + \beta'_{w_3 i} \Delta S_{it} +$$

$$\beta'_{b_4 i} P_i +$$

$$\beta'_{b_5 i} \overline{D}_i * \overline{S}_i + \beta'_{w_5 i} \Delta D_{it} * \Delta S_i +$$

$$\beta'_{b_6 i} \overline{D}_i * P_i + \beta'_{b_6 i} \Delta D_{it} * P_i +$$

$$\beta'_{b_7 i} \overline{S}_i * P_i + \beta'_{w_6 i} \Delta S_{it} * P +$$

$$\beta'_{b_8 i} \overline{D}_i * \overline{S}_i * P_i + \beta'_{w_8 i} \Delta D_{it} * \Delta S_i * P_i + u_{it}$$

(eq. 8)

Since an interaction between the within-person term for delinquency (or drug use) and sanctions is included in the model, the interaction term of delinquency and the sanction gives the effect of the interaction for middle-class youth who experienced the sanction. The three way interaction shows how much the moderating effects of suspension or arrest on delinquency or drug use is offset by being poor. A negative interaction term for the three-way interaction would indicate that being suspended or arrested matters less for poor than for non-poor youth.

CHAPTER 4

Explaining Drug Use, Delinquency, and Dropout

DESCRIPTIVE FINDINGS

Figure 4-1 gives two different types of dropout rates. First, Figure 4-1 gives the proportion of youth in the NLSY97 who were dropouts at each interview (referred to as "dropout status"). Second, since dropouts may reenroll in school, Figure 3 gives the proportion of youth who had ever dropped out by each interview, regardless of whether they ever returned. This is referred to as "cumulative dropout." Since the data are weighted, the dropout rates can be thought of as generalizable to the population of U.S. youth born between 1980 and 1984.[12] As can be seen, in round 1, most NLSY97 youth were not yet dropouts. Only 2.4 percent of youth were dropouts at the time of the round 1 interview. Looking at the "dropout status" curve, at round 7, 17.9 percent of youth were dropouts. The "cumulative dropout" curve shows that by round 7, 23.2 percent of youth had ever dropped out of school at some point. Therefore, dropping out is not an uncommon experience for youth in the NLSY97. It is worth noting that cumulative dropout is somewhat higher than dropout status at each round. This indicates that dropping out is a temporary situation for many youth. Since GEDs are counted as dropouts here, the lower current dropout status cannot reflect youth who are obtaining GEDs. Rather, it represents dropouts who apparently reenroll in school.

Figure 4-1. Proportion of dropouts, by survey year

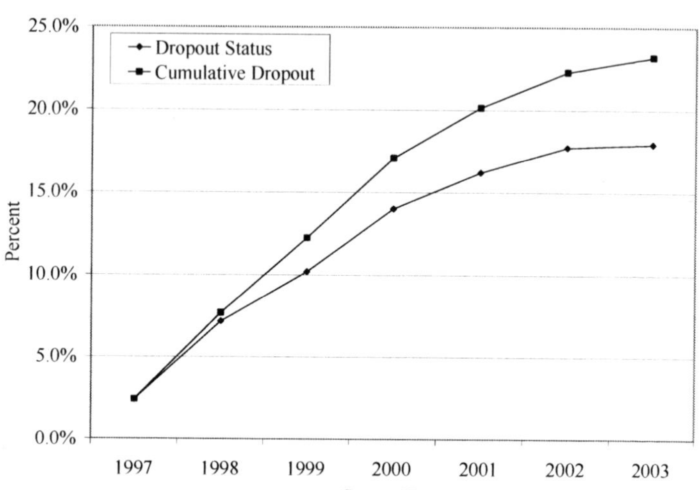

Figure 4-2 presents the same two dropout rates for poor and non-poor youth separately. When the curves are broken out separately by poverty status, it is clear that dropping out is a problem that is highly concentrated among youth who were living in poverty in 1996. At round 7, 37.0 percent of poor youth were dropouts, and 45.2 percent had ever dropped out. Among youth who were not poor, 14 percent were dropouts at round 7 and 18.9 percent had ever dropped out. Therefore, while youth who are not poor do drop out of school, they do so at a much lower rate than do poor youth. The Appendix provides a more detailed look at dropout rates by survey year as well as age.

Table A-9 presents descriptive statistics for delinquency and drug use. Several different descriptive statistics on delinquency and drug use are presented. All descriptive statistics are presented for the sample as a whole and for poor and non-poor youth separately. Information on both the prevalence and variety of delinquency is given. The column labeled "pooled" gives the percentage of person-year observations in which a behavior was occurred (prevalence). Delinquency is quite common, occurring in 28.8 percent of the person-years. Looking at the year specific estimates, the prevalence of delinquency decreases over time. In 1997, 48.9 percent of youth had committed an offense. In

1998, 32.8 percent had committed an offense, and 27.6 percent had committed an offense in 1999. By 2002, only 18.3 percent of youth committed any delinquency. However, delinquency is still quite common among the sample. The within-person column gives the percent of youth who ever engaged in delinquency at any time across all of the interviews. As can be seen, about two-thirds of youth (66.7 percent) participate in delinquency at least once across the waves in which they were observed.

Figure 4-2. Proportion of dropouts, by survey year and poverty status

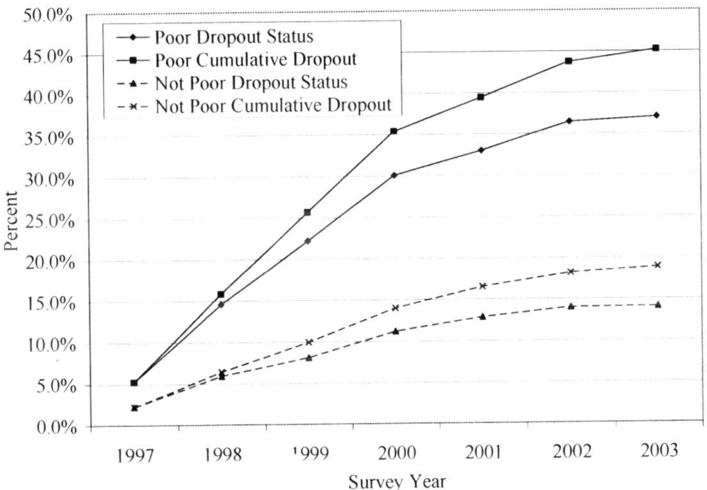

The mean number of different offenses (or mean variety) is calculated only for youth who reported engaging in delinquency. The pooled column shows that in the person-year observations in which delinquency occurred, an average of 2.95 different offenses were committed. The annual estimates show that among youth who engaged in some delinquency, the number of different offenses decreases over time alongside the prevalence. In 1997, youth who committed any delinquency engaged in an average of 3.00 different offenses. In 2002, offenders committed an average of 2.59 different offenses. The within-person column for variety gives the average number of different offenses committed by a youth in the years in which they committed any delinquency. A youth who committed any delinquency committed an average of 2.59 different offenses in the years in which they offended.

Drug use is also more common than delinquency, with youth engaging in at least one of the seven drug use behaviors in 53.8 percent of the person-year observations. In contrast to delinquency, drug use tends to increase over time. In round 1, 27.2 percent of youth had used any drugs. In round 7, 71.1 percent of youth had used drugs. The within-person column shows that 84.0 percent of youth had ever used drugs. The variety of drug use also increases over time.

Small differences were found between poor and non-poor youth in terms of delinquency and drug use. Youth who were living in poverty were slightly more delinquent than youth who were not living in poverty. For example, the within-person column shows that 70.1 percent of poor youth committed delinquency at least once compared to 66.0 percent of non-poor youth. The average variety estimates also show that when poor youth commit delinquency, they commit a wider variety of offenses compared to non-poor youth. In terms of drug use, the difference is in the opposite direction: poor youth use drugs less than non-poor youth. For example, the within-person column shows that 80.5 percent of poor youth used drugs at least once, and 84.7 percent of non-poor youth used at least once. When non-poor youth do use drugs, they also use a wider variety of substances. That is to say, drug use appears to be more common among non-poor youth, although again the difference is not large.

Table A-10 shows differences between dropouts and non-dropouts in terms of the independent variables used in the study. To avoid confusion that might result from the use of pooled data, differences are presented for dropouts in 1998 based on 1997 characteristics. Results are again broken out by poverty status. The first column presents results for all youth. In terns of demographics, dropouts are more likely than non-dropouts to be black and Hispanic and less likely to be white and Asian. Dropouts are more likely to have parents who themselves dropped out of high school or completed only high school and are less likely to have parents who graduated from college. They also come from families that have lower incomes. Dropouts are also more likely to have been born of a teenage mother. Family structure is also related to dropping out. Youth who come from parental family structures other than two-parent biological families are more likely to drop out. There is no difference in the probability of dropping out based on coming from an urban or rural area. Dropouts also perceive their mothers' as being more permissive (as opposed to strict), and come from households where moving is more frequent.

Table A-10 also shows that dropping out is not just associated with a youth's social background but also with his or her school experiences. Dropouts have lower grades in middle school than non-dropouts and are much more likely to have repeated a grade. Dropouts also change schools more frequently, have lower cognitive ability test scores, and have greater exposure to deviant youth in school and less exposure to more conventionally oriented peers.

Table A-10 also shows that taking on adult roles prematurely is also related to dropping out. Dropouts are more likely to have given birth to a child, are more likely to have worked, are more likely to be living with a sexual partner, and are more likely to have had sex. The difference in sexual intercourse prevalence is quite striking. Over half (56.1 percent) of dropouts have had sex, versus 18.2 percent of non-dropouts. These findings generally confirm those of prior studies showing that dropouts are more socioeconomically disadvantaged, have more problems at home and at school, and take on adult roles earlier.

Table A-10 breaks out the analysis by poverty status. Several interesting results emerge when this is done. Socioeconomic background factors—including race, income, parental education, and family structure—do not distinguish dropouts from non-dropouts among poor youth as well as they do among non-poor youth. This is not surprising, given that the majority of poor dropouts are already disadvantaged and tend to fit the mold of the "typical" high school dropout. However, among non-poor youth, family structure is related to dropout. This is because whereas poor youth tend to come from single parent families, this is not necessarily the case for non-poor youth. Both groups appear to be disadvantaged in terms of academics.

Table A-11 shows how delinquency in round 1 is associated with dropout status in round 2. Among the full sample, dropouts are more likely to have participated in delinquency in the past year than non-dropouts (61.5 percent versus 47.8 percent). Among youth who participated in any delinquency, dropouts also committed a wider variety of offenses than did non-dropouts on average (4.07 versus 2.90). When the relationship between delinquency and dropout is examined separately for the 21 individual offenses, dropouts are more likely to have participated in nearly every offense. Note also that the largest differences between dropout and non-dropouts are in terms of their participation in the most serious offenses. Dropouts are more than twice as likely to have committed an aggravated assault in the past year (34.5 percent versus 14.4 percent), and about one third more likely to have committed petty theft (40.8 percent versus 30.6 percent). It should be noted, however, that delinquency is still very common among non-dropouts and that not all youth who participate in delinquency drop out of school.

When the relationship between delinquency and dropout is examined separately for poor and non-poor youth, it is clear that poor dropouts are less involved in delinquency than are non-poor dropouts. For example, 58.6 percent of poor dropouts committed delinquency in the past year compared to 68.6 percent of non-poor dropouts. When differences in the 21 individual offenses are examined, these differences in participation are limited to relatively minor offenses. Poor dropouts are more likely to commit relatively serious offenses, whereas non-poor dropouts are more likely to commit relatively minor offenses. For example, 22.3 percent of poor dropouts carried a handgun—a relatively serious offense—compared to 15.1 percent of non-poor dropouts. On the other hand, 33.3 percent of non-poor dropouts committed petty theft—a relatively minor offense—compared to 44.7 percent of poor dropouts. Delinquency is more strongly associated with dropout among middle-class than among poor youth, although this tends to be the case more for minor than for serious offenses.

Table A-12 shows that drug use is also strongly associated with dropping out. Dropouts are almost twice as likely to have engaged in any drug use in the past month than are non-dropouts (52.6 percent versus 25.4 percent). Among youth who are involved in drug use, dropouts participate is wider variety of different behaviors than do non-dropouts (4.07 versus 2.90).. Looking at the seven individual drug use measures separately reveals that regardless of the type of use, drug use is linked with dropout. The largest differences in drug use between dropouts and non-dropouts are in terms of cigarette smoking (44.0 percent versus 15.5 percent) and using marijuana before or during school or work (9.5 percent versus 2.8 percent).

Poor dropouts are slightly less involved in drug use than non-poor dropouts, although these differences are quite small. For example, 51.9 percent of poor dropouts used drugs, relative to 52.9 percent of non-poor dropouts. When dropouts do use drugs, there is no difference between poor and non-poor dropouts in terms of the number of different drugs they use (2.49 versus 2.49). There are some differences by drug type. While poor dropouts are more likely to smoke cigarettes and to do so more heavily than are non-poor dropouts, they are less likely to binge drink, use marijuana, and use marijuana before or during school or work.

RESULTS FROM PANEL MODELS

Delinquency Predicting Dropout

I first present results without considering the possible role of social class or mediating mechanisms in order to assess the effects of delinquency and drug use on dropout overall. Since delinquency and drug use are highly correlated, three separate sets of models are run. The first set of models includes delinquency as a predictor, the second set of models includes drug use as a predictor, and the third set of models includes both delinquency and drug use as predictors. Table A-13 reports the results from the logistic regression models predicting dropout from past year delinquency variety. Models were run in several steps. Models 1 and 2 are not random or fixed effects models but rather "conventional" logistic regression models, which attempt to equate youth who differ in their levels of delinquency (or drug use) by including controls for selection in the form of observed covariates. These models strictly assume that there are no unobserved differences between youth which might account for the relationships among delinquency, drug use, and dropping out. All of the models include dummy variables for survey year, age, region of residence, birth cohort, and the number of months that have elapsed since the last interview. To account for the clustered nature of the data, standard errors are corrected for clustering at the individual and household levels.

These models indicate whether delinquency is associated with dropout, net of the control variables included in the model. Model 1 includes only a measure of delinquency variety from the past year and shows the expected positive and significant relationship between delinquency and dropout. Youth who are more involved in delinquency are more likely to be dropouts. The coefficient of .141 indicates that increasing participation in delinquency by one type of offense increases the odds of dropout 15.1 [(exp(.141)-1)*100] percent. Youth who commit two offenses have an odds of dropout that are 32.5

[(exp(.141*2)-1)*100] percent higher than youth who did not commit any delinquency.

Model 2, which is also a "conventional" logistic regression model, adds all of the observed control variables in an effort to determine the relative importance of delinquency for dropout. In Model 2, the coefficient for delinquency is reduced by over 50 percent but is still highly significant. Committing one type of offense increases the odds of dropout 5.9 [(exp(.057)-1)*100] percent. Committing two types of offenses increases the odds of dropout by 12.1 [(exp(.057*2)-1)*100] percent.

The findings for the association of many of the control variables and dropout replicate those of prior studies on dropout. In terms of demographic background, being male is strongly associated with dropout. Both parental education and household income are independently associated with dropout, indicating that it is both human capital and parents' knowledge of how to navigate the school system that are important for dropout. It is interesting to note that once these measures of socioeconomic status are controlled, Hispanic youth are no more likely than white youth to be dropouts and black youth are less likely than white youth to be dropouts. This finding suggests that the high dropout rates of minority youth are largely a function of their socioeconomic background, a finding which has been documented by other studies (Fernandez, Paulsen, and Hirano-Nakanishi 1989; Hauser, Simmons, and Pager 2004; Plank, DeLuca, and Estacion 2008). Family structure, particularly living with a single mother or father or with other adults, is also strongly associated with dropout, as is a history of frequent residential mobility before age 12.

Not surprisingly, many of the school experience variables are strongly related to dropout, even in the presence of the myriad control variables. Low middle school grades, repeating a grade, and low attachment to school are all associated with dropout, as are low ASVAB scores and exposure to antisocial peers at school. The association between ever repeating a grade and dropout is among the strongest in the table. Youth who are held back a grade have odds of dropping out 161.7 [(exp(.962)-1)*100] percent more likely to drop out than youth who never repeated a grade. Changing schools is also strongly associated with being a dropout.

Finally, engaging in deviant behaviors other than delinquency and drug use and adult role transitions are also strongly associated with dropout net of the included control variables. Having sexual intercourse, having a child, working an average of more than 20 hours per week, and living with an opposite sex partner are all associated with dropout, all other things being equal. Some of these relationships are among the strongest in the table, perhaps only second to grade retention. For example, the odds of dropout for youth who have ever had sex are 131.2 [(exp(.843)-1)*100] higher as than for youth who have not had sex. The odds of dropout for youth who have had a child are 338 [(exp(1.477)-1)*100] percent higher than for youth who have never had a child. Since childbearing is controlled in the model, this suggests that the effect of precocious sexual intercourse is not due to its effect on having children.

While Model 2 is a significant improvement over much prior research on delinquency and dropout in that it controls for a wide array of predictors of both delinquency and dropout, it is still vulnerable to criticisms of selection bias, as there may be unobserved characteristics driving the relationship between delinquency and dropout. To help address this possibility, Model 3 is the first of two models that addresses selection on observed as well as unobserved characteristics. Model 3 is the "hybrid" random effects logit model. This model provides my first key test of whether the relationship between prior delinquency and later dropout is attributable to preexisting differences. I begin by examining the "between" coefficients, which give the average between-person differences in dropout for youth with different levels of delinquency averaged across all survey waves. Consistent with the findings from Model 2, the between-person coefficient for delinquency is positive and significant and similar in magnitude to what it was in the model with controls. This suggests a strong association between delinquency and dropout at the between-person level. That is, youth with higher levels of delinquency are more likely to be dropouts than youth with lower levels of delinquency.

My main interest, however, is the "within" coefficient, which gives the change in dropout status (from in school to dropout or vice versa) that follows from a change (increase or decrease) in delinquency and provides the best evidence of a causal effect of delinquency on dropout net of time-invariant individual differences. The within-person coefficient for prior delinquency is close to zero and non-significant. *This means that although youth with higher levels of delinquency are more likely to be dropouts, as evidenced in the "between" coefficient, changes in delinquency do not lead to changes in dropout status in the following year. Rather, the association between delinquency and dropout is attributable to unobserved between-person differences that predispose youth to both behaviors. Youth who are more heavily involved in delinquency are more likely to be dropouts, but not because they are involved in delinquency.* This finding is consistent with prior studies that have found that delinquency is not a good predictor of dropout once other predictors of dropout are controlled (Fagan and Pabon 1990; Krohn et al. 1995)

While my main interest is in the effects of delinquency, it is interesting to examine the effects of the other predictor variables in the random effects models. In the model that includes only observed controls for selection, many of the predictor variables are highly significant. However, not all of these variables have significant within-person effects in the random effects model. While family structure was related to dropout, changes in family structure do not appear to be related to changes in dropout. However, repeating a grade does appear to lead to dropping out. It is also interesting to note that changing schools, which was not associated with dropout, does have a significant within-person effect. Although youth who drop out are more likely to be parents, this effect does not appear to be causal. This suggests that youth who drop out may have children after dropping out, or some unobserved characteristic—such as dissatisfaction with school—may be driving the decision to have children and to discontinue education. On the other hand, working while in school, although the effect is reduced from the conventional logistic model, is strongly related to dropping out, as is initiating sexual behavior.

Figure 4-3 plots the predicted probability of dropout at each survey year by delinquency. These predicted probabilities are derived from the random effects model, specifically, the within-person coefficients for delinquency. All of the control variables are held constant at their mean levels, including the between-person effects. For within-person coefficients, the mean is naturally zero, since the average deviation of an individual's score from his or her average is equal to zero. For between-person effects, the mean is the average level of the variable first average within individual and then average across individuals. This strategy ensured that the between-person mean did not overweight individuals with greater number of person-year observations. As can be seen, the differences in the predicted probabilities of dropout are small, even for large changes in delinquency. For example, in 1998, the predicted probability of dropout for an average youth who commits no delinquent offenses the prior year is 6.7 percent. For a youth who commits 5 offenses the prior year but who is the same on all other characteristics, the predicted probability is virtually the same—6.9 percent. This, along with the "within-person" estimate for the effects of delinquency, suggests that delinquency is not an important contributor to dropping out of school.

Figure 4-3. Predicted probability of dropout from hybrid random effects model, by delinquency

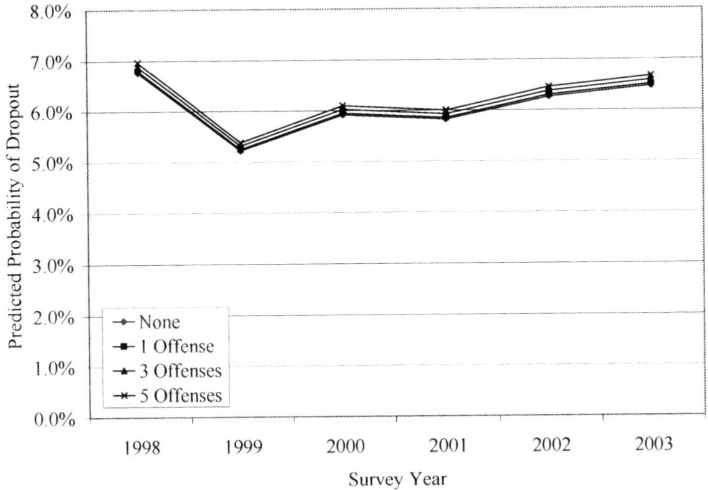

In sum, the results of the panel models presented in this section indicate that although youth who are more involved in delinquency are more likely to drop out of school than are youth who are less involved or not involved at all in delinquency, this is not necessarily because delinquency is *causally* related to dropping out of school. Rather, the relationship between delinquency and dropout appears to be spurious, owing to preexisting differences that drive youth to commit delinquency and to drop out. While delinquency in these results does not appear to be important for dropping out, other factors, such as repeating a grade or taking on adult roles, such as working or having sex, do contribute to a youth's decision to drop out, even when preexisting differences are taken into account.

Drug Use Predicting Dropout

Table A-14 presents the results from the logistic regressions of dropout in relation to prior drug use. The model steps are the same as for delinquency in the previous section. Model 1 includes only past month frequency of drug use. The coefficient for prior drug use is positive and highly significant, indicating that higher frequencies of drug use are positively associated with dropout. Each additional increase in the drug use variety scale increases the odds of being a dropout 24.5 [(exp(.219)-1)*100] percent. The odds of being a dropout for youth who engage in two of the drug use behaviors is 55.0 [(exp(.219*2)-1)*100] higher than youth who do not use drugs. The association between drug use and dropout at the bivariate level is therefore very strong relative to that for delinquency.

Model 2 adds all of the observed controls for selection. The coefficient for drug use is reduced by 17.7 percent (100-(.181/.219)) when all of the control variables are included, although it is still highly significant and large. With all of the control variables included, increasing drug use participation by one behavior increases the odds of dropout 19.8 [(exp(.181*1)-1)*100] percent.

Model 3 is the hybrid random effects models, which controls for both observed and unobserved sources of selection. The between-person coefficient is positive and highly significant, indicating that youth with higher levels of drug use are more likely to be dropouts. The within-person coefficient is also significant, although substantially reduced in magnitude. This suggests that although drug use and dropping out share causes, drug use still exerts an effect on dropping out, with increases in drug use leading to dropping out of school the following year. For example, each additional increase of one drug use behavior increases the odds of dropping out by about 5.8 [(exp(.056)-1)*100] percent.

Figure 4-4 plots the predicted probability of dropout for different levels of drug use from the random effects model. Predicted probabilities are plotted for each survey year. As can be seen, the differences in the predicted probabilities for different levels of drug use, while statistically significant, are small in size. For example, in 1998, the predicted probability of transitioning from being enrolled to being a dropout is 6.6 percent for youth who did not report using any drugs in the month preceding the survey. For youth who changed from using no drugs to using three different drugs, the predicted probability is 7.5 percent. For youth who report changing from no drug use to the max level of the scale—7 different drug use activities—the predicted probability is 9.0 percent. Therefore, while changes in drug use are significantly associated with changes in dropping out, these changes are quite small. This findings is in line with those of prior studies that have found small but significant effects of drug use on dropout (Friedman et al. 1983; Kaplan and Liu 1994). Drug use may increase the risk of dropout, but it may not be the most important factor in why youth drop out of school.

Figure 4-4. Predicted probability of dropout from hybrid random effects model, by drug use

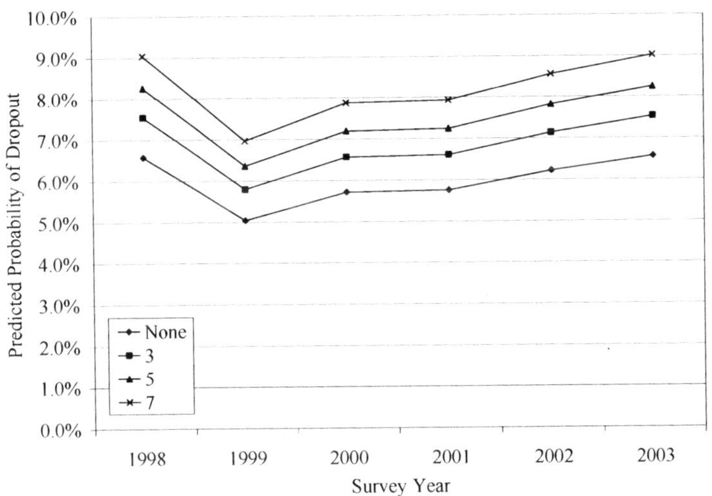

In sum, the results of the models for drug use predicting dropout indicate that drug use and dropout do share causes. However, drug use leads to dropout over and above common causes. It is important to note, however, that the effects of drug use are modest, with an increase from no use to daily use increasing the odds of dropout 19 percent. Other predictors of dropout—in particular, changing residences, repeating a grade, working more than 20 hours per week, and having sex—have much larger effects. These results are different, however, than those obtained for delinquency. Although youth with higher levels of participation in delinquency are more likely to be dropouts, increasing delinquency does not lead to a change in dropout status. Instead, prior delinquency and later dropping out appear to be spuriously related. This finding is in agreement with prior studies that have found fragile effects of delinquency once other variables are controlled. Overall, these findings suggest that drug use, but not delinquency, leads to dropping out of school, but also that the effects associated with drug use are quite modest.

Delinquency and Drug Use Predicting Dropout

Because delinquency and drug use co-occur, it is important to examine the relative importance of the two behaviors for predicting dropout simultaneously. Table A-15 gives the results from the same logistic regression models in the previous sections, this time predicting dropout status with both delinquency and drug use included at the same time. Model 1 includes only delinquency and drug use predicting dropout. The coefficients for both prior delinquency and drug use are positive and significant, indicating that each is uniquely associated with dropout. However, the coefficient for delinquency is much smaller than it was in the models that did not include drug use, indicating that drug is is picking up some of the effect of delinquency.

When observed controls for selection are included in Model 2, the coefficients for delinquency and drug use are still positive and significant, although substantially reduced.

Model 3 is the random effects model. The within-person coefficient for delinquency is not significantly different from zero, but the within-person coefficient for drug use remains positive and highly significant. The magnitude of the drug use effect is similar to what it was in the models that included only drug use. This suggests that when youth are involved in both behaviors, drug use supersedes delinquency as a predictor of dropping out.

To sum up, the results of models that include *both* delinquency and drug use predicting dropping out indicate that the association between delinquency and dropping out is at least partially due to drug use. That is, when youth who are involved in delinquency drop out of high school, it is at least partially due to the fact that delinquency and drug use tend to co-occur and that drug use is driving the relationship. This finding is in line with Krohn et al. (1995) and others who have found that delinquency is a rather fragile predictor of dropping out once drug use is included in multivariate statistical models.

<u>Sensitivity Analyses: The Effects of Delinquency and Drug Use</u>
In this section, I present the results from several sensitivity analyses I conducted to determine whether the findings from the previous section change if different assumptions are made about the effects of delinquency and drug use on dropout. One possibility is that the effects of delinquency and drug use on dropping out are not the same for all types of delinquency or drug use. For example, aggravated assault may illicit a more serious reaction from school officials or police than petty shoplifting or vandalism. Similarly, smoking cigarettes might not be as detrimental to cognitive ability and hence school performance as binge drinking or using marijuana. To investigate whether such differences affect the findings, I reran all of the logistic regression models separately for each individual delinquency and drug use indicator rather than for the omnibus delinquency and drug use scales. All analyses were conducted using the individual behavior prevalence (committed versus did not commit) as well as the frequency of the behaviors for the limited number of behaviors for which frequency was available. The results of these analyses are summarized in Table A-16 for delinquency and Table A-17 for drug use.

The left panel of 16 presents the results for the prevalence of the specific delinquent offenses, and the right panel reports on the frequency for the offenses which had frequency information available. Models 1 through 3 are the same three models that were presented in the previous sections. Model 1 is the conventional logistic regression model run on the person-year and includes only whether the youth committed the specific offense in the past year as a predictor (plus dummies for survey year, age, region, birth cohort, and a continuous variable for months elapsed since the last interview or since birth in round 1). To ease presentation, coefficients are not presented. Rather, positive and statistically significant coefficients at the .05 level are denoted with a "+." Negative and statistically significant coefficients at the .05 level are denoted with a "-." Non-significant coefficients are denoted with "NS." As can be seen when looking at the left panel for prevalence, when no controls are included in the model, all 21 delinquent offenses are strongly related to dropout. Model 2 is also a conventional logistic regression but, as before, includes all of the observed controls to capture pre-existing differences between youth. The coefficients for all but three of the delinquent offenses—petty shoplifting, petty larceny, and major larceny—are still significant. In Model 3, which is the random effects model, all of the between-person coefficients for the specific offenses are positive and significant, but none of the within-person coefficients are significant. Looking at the right panel for the frequency of the specific offenses, although many of the between-person coefficients are positive and significant, none of the within-person estimates reach statistical significance. This confirms the finding in the previous sections that while delinquency is related to dropout, changes in delinquency do not lead to changes in dropout. Even at the level of specific offenses, the pattern is the same.

Table A-17 summarizes the results from similar set of analyses for drug use. In Model 1, which includes no controls, the coefficients for six of the seven drug use indicators are positive and statistically significant. The only coefficient that is not statistically significant is for alcohol use. This may have to do with the fact that alcohol is the most commonly used drug among youth in the NLSY97. As early as round 1, over 75 percent of youth reported having used alcohol. Alcohol use may be too common to distinguish dropouts from non-dropouts. Alcohol use *per se* does not appear to be associated with dropout. In Model 2, when the observed controls are included, the coefficients for all of the six drug use indicators are still positive and significant. The coefficient for alcohol use is still non-significant. Model 3 is the random effects model. The between-person coefficients for the six drug use indicators are all positive and significant, as expected. However, there are some differences when the within-person coefficients are examined. Two of the within-person coefficients—the one for smoking cigarettes and the one for using marijuana—are positive and significant. This indicates that changing from not smoking cigarettes to smoking cigarettes or from not using marijuana to using marijuana are both associated with changes in dropout status.[13]

The second column of Table A-17 presents results using the frequency of drug use for the indicators for which frequency information was available. Frequency information was available for all of the drug use indicators except smoking more than 1 pack of cigarettes per day. In Model 3, which is the most stringent specification, smoking cigarettes and using marijuana again have effects on dropout. However, changes in the frequency of binge drinking are also positively associated with changes in dropout. It is not simply drinking alcohol or even drinking large quantities of alcohol but rather drinking large quantities of alcohol *frequently* that negatively impacts school persistence.

A second issue that needs to be examined is whether the effects of delinquency and drug use operate in ways that are different from those specified in the models in the previous sections. The models presented in the previous sections assume that an increase in the delinquency or drug use has the same effect on dropout at all levels of delinquency or drug use. For example, it is assumed that a shift from committing any delinquency to one offense has the same consequences for dropout, all other things being equal, as a shift from 10 offenses to 11 offenses. Clearly, both of these things are not the same, and there is no reason to assume that the effects of delinquency or drug use would be the same in both cases. To examine this issue further, I again reran all of the models, this time using different polynomial specifications for the effects of delinquency and drug use and specifying delinquency and drug use as a series of categorical dummy variables.

The results of these analyses are summarized in Table A-18 for delinquency and in Table A-19 for drug use. Results are presented for the variety scale and for the frequency scale separately, but the latter only includes the more limited number of behaviors for which frequency was available. Looking at Table A-18 for delinquency, the first alternative model specification was a quadratic one, which involved including a squared term for delinquency. This modeling specification explores whether there is a curvilinear association or effect of delinquency on dropout. That is, increasing participation in delinquency may matter for dropout at lower but not higher levels of participation. As in previous analyses, the same three models were run. Model 1 includes the quadratic specification with no control variables (except dummies for survey year, age, region, and birth year, and exposure time). As can be seen, the coefficient for the delinquency squared term is negative and significant, indicating that the strength of the association between delinquency and dropout increases, peaks, and then declines. This indicates that differences in delinquency at the lower end of the scale are more important for distinguishing dropouts from non-dropouts than are differences in delinquency at the higher end of the scale. However, when observed and unobserved controls for selection are added in Models 2 and 3, respectively, both the "main effect" and curvature parameters drop from significance. Similar results were obtained for the frequency scale.

Binary and ordinal specifications of the effects of delinquency were also examined. The first was a binary delinquency variable— coded 1 if a youth committed any delinquency and 0 if they committed no delinquency since the last interview. In Models 1 and 2, the coefficient for this variable is positive and significant, indicating that committing any delinquency is related to dropout. However, in Model 3, the between-person coefficient but not the within-person coefficient for binary delinquency variable is significant. This indicates that youth who participate in delinquency are more likely to be dropouts, but that switching from no delinquency to any delinquency does not lead to changes in dropout status.

An ordinal specification coded delinquency as a categorical set of dummy variables with non-offenders treated as the reference category. Since the variety and frequency scales are in different units, different ordinal specifications are created for each scale. Looking at the results for the variety scale, the positive and significant coefficients from Models 1 and 2 show that youth who commit 1 to 3 offenses, 4 to 6 offenses, 7 to 9 offenses, 9 to 12 offenses, and more than 12 offenses are all more likely to be dropouts than are non-offenders. However, once unobserved between-person controls for selection are included in Model 3, consistent with the findings in previous sections, none of the delinquency coefficients corresponding to these categories is significant. Similar results are obtained for the categorical frequency dummy variables.

Another potential criticism of my findings, particularly for delinquency, is that my models assume that delinquency and drug use have effects on dropout over a relatively short time period— specifically, within 1 year. It may be that the effects of delinquency and drug use on dropout take longer to manifest. To examine whether delinquency and drug use have long-term effects on dropout, I again estimated the same three models, this time including a different lag structure. Specifically, I included simultaneously three different delinquency (and drug use) variables in the models. The first was delinquency in the past year, which is the same measure I included in the previous models. The second was delinquency measured two years ago, and the third was delinquency measured three years ago. Looking at the results in the left panel for delinquency variety, Model 3 shows that the within-person coefficients for delinquency from one, two, and three years ago are not statistically significant. However, in Model 3 for the frequency of delinquency, the within-person coefficient for delinquency from three years ago is positive and significant, while the coefficients for the shorter lags (two and one year ago) are indistinguishable from zero. This provides some evidence of a long-term effect of delinquency on dropout.[14]

Finally, although the variety scale is less skewed than the frequency scale, it is still not normally distributed. It is therefore important to rule out the possibility that the findings are being driven by a few outliers with a high level of delinquency. To investigate this, I conducted two different analyses. First, I top-coded the delinquency variable at various levels and reran all of the models to see whether this changed the findings. For the variety scale, which had a maximum value of 21, I top-coded values at 15, 10, and 5 offenses. For the frequency scale, I top-coded values at 50, 40, 30, 20, and 10 times. As can be seen, top-coding had no effect on the findings for either the delinquency or variety scales. In a second analysis, I logged the delinquency variable to draw in the tail. (This strategy has the added benefit of reducing the problem discussed earlier of the assumption that the effects of delinquency are the same at all levels of delinquency.) As can be seen, logging the delinquency measure did not alter the findings. Similar results for analyses performed on the frequency scale are presented in the right panel.

Table A-19 summarizes an analogous set of analyses for drug use. In the results for the quadratic specification for drug use, the curvature parameter is negative and significant in Models 1 and 2, but the within-person coefficient is not significant in Model 3. Results for binary and ordinal specifications are also presented. Changing from no drug use to any use is associated with changes in dropout. Looking at the ordinal specification for variety, we see that changing from 0 to 1 or 2 drug use incidents is not associated with changes in dropout in Model 3. Moreover, looking at the right panel for frequency, the results of the ordinal specification, Model 3 indicates that increases in drug use from no use to 15 times per month or less are not associated with changes in dropout. Only changes from no use to higher frequency of use—specifically, more than 15 times per month—is associated with dropout. This indicates that it is not drug use *per se* that is related to dropout, but rather frequent drug use, an effect that is somewhat obscured by the variety measure (although the variety measure is strongly correlated with frequency and does pick up some frequency effects).

Results from the models that include one, two, and three year lagged measures of drug use indicate that for frequency, only drug use in the past year leads to dropout. Earlier drug use (two and three years ago) has no effect on dropout over and above more contemporaneous drug use. Results for drug use variety indicate that none of the different lagged measures has an effect on dropout.[15]

This finding is further confirmed in the top-coded analyses, in which the frequency of drug use capped at 30 has no effect on dropout. When capped at higher levels—60 and 90—changes in drug use are associated with changes in dropout. (Variety was not top-coded since the highest value was 7.) Again, this indicates that it is only frequent drug use that is important for dropout.[16]

To sum up, the results of the sensitivity analyses conducted in this section shed some further light on the effects of delinquency and drug use on dropout. In terms of delinquency, the sensitivity analyses indicate that the finding that delinquency does not lead to dropout holds up when the 21 delinquent offenses are considered separately and when a variety of different modeling assumptions are tested. There is some evidence of a possible long-term effect of delinquency, but this finding should be interpreted with caution given the possible unrepresentative nature of dropouts included in the sample. For drug use, when examining the specific indicators, the findings indicate that alcohol use *per se* has no effect on dropping out, but rather that frequent, heavy use of alcohol is the relevant condition. In addition, the findings indicate that beginning to use drugs at low frequencies—namely, less than 15 times per month—is not associated with changes in dropout. Rather, it is changing to higher levels of drug use—more than 15 times per month—that is associated with changes in dropout. Moreover, there is some evidence that these effects of frequent drug use are time-limited: increases in drug use lead to dropout the next year. Early drug use is important once past month drug use is taken into account.

The Role of Social Class

<u>Do delinquency and drug use have different effects on dropout for youth from different social classes?</u>
Having examined the overall impact of delinquency and drug use on dropout, I now turn my attention to my second research question: Do delinquency and drug use have different effects on dropout for youth from different social classes? To answer this question, I reran the same three logistic regression models as in previous sections, this time including interactions between delinquency and drug use and the measure of poverty status. Table A-20 gives the results from these analyses for delinquency. As in prior tables, Model 1 does not include

any substantive controls. As can be seen, the coefficient for the "main effect" of delinquency is positive and statistically significant. Since the model includes an interaction between delinquency and poverty status, the coefficient for delinquency gives the association between delinquency and dropout when poverty status is equal to 0. In other words, the coefficient for delinquency gives the association between delinquency and dropout for non-poor youth only. For non-poor youth, each delinquent offense increases the odds of dropout 17.2 [(exp(.159)-1)*100] percent. To get the odds for poor youth, we need to focus on both the interaction term and the "main effect" of delinquency. The coefficient for the interaction between delinquency and poverty status is negative and statistically significant. This indicates that delinquency is less strongly associated with dropout for poor youth than it is for non-poor youth. For poor youth, each delinquent offense increases the odds of dropout 12.3 [(exp(.159-.043)-1)*100] percent.

Model 2 adds all of the observed controls, as in previous sections. The interaction between delinquency and poverty status, while still negative, is not significantly different from zero after the control variables have been included. This indicates that the control variables account for the difference in delinquency between poor and non-poor dropouts. The results from Model 3—the random effects model—are the same. The interaction between the within-person delinquency component and poverty status is not statistically significant. Therefore, while delinquency and dropout are more strongly associated among non-poor youth, this relationship does not appear to be a causal one. Changes in delinquency do not lead to dropout for non-poor youth. At the same time, changes in delinquency also do not lead to dropout for poor youth. Non-poor dropouts are more likely to be involved in delinquency, but delinquency contributes little to dropping out for either group once strong controls for between-person differences are included.

Table A-21 gives the results for logistic regression models of drug use predicting dropout including an interaction between drug use and poverty status. In Model 1, the coefficient for drug use indicates the relationship between drug use and dropout for non-poor youth. For non-poor youth, a one unit increase in the drug use variety scale increases the odds of dropout 26.8 [(exp(.238)-1)*100] percent. The interaction between drug use and poverty status is not significantly different from zero, however, indicating that there is no difference in the relationship between drug use and dropout between non-poor and poor youth, a finding which is consistent with the smaller descriptive differences in drug use between the two groups presented earlier. For poor youth, the odds of dropout associated with a one behavior increase in the drug use variety scale is 27.3 [(exp(.238+.004)-1)*100] percent, which is not different from the odds for non-poor youth.

This finding is unchanged by the results from Models 2, although the overall effect of drug use is reduced by the inclusion of control variables. In Model 3, the within-person coefficient for drug use is positive and significant, indicating that changes in drug use are associated with changes in dropout among non-poor youth. The interaction between the within-person coefficient for drug use and poverty status indicates that this effect does not differ by social class. Increasing drug use variety by one behavior leads to an increase in the odds of dropout for non-poor youth of 5.7 [(exp(.055)-1)*100] percent. For poor youth, the same increase in drug use leads to an increase in the odds of dropout of 4.1 [(exp(.055-.015)-1)*100] percent, a difference which is not significantly different. Drug use leads to dropout for both poor and non-poor youth.

To sum up, while delinquency and drug use are less common among poor than among non-poor dropouts, the results of the analyses presented in this section provide no evidence that the effects of delinquency or drug use on dropout depend on a youth's social class. For both poor and non-poor youth, delinquency has no effect on dropout. However, drug use has effects on dropout for both poor and non-poor youth. As I will investigate later, however, the fact that delinquency does not lead to dropout for either social class does not mean that the underlying explanation for why delinquency is associated with dropout is the same for the two groups.

<u>Sensitivity Analysis: The Role of Social Class</u>
One concern about my findings is that the non-poverty group is actually quite large and diverse. Variability within this group could be masking interaction effects between delinquency (or drug use) and social class. To investigate this possibility, I constructed an ordinal rather than binary measure of social class that indicates how much a youth's household income differs from (or is greater than) the poverty line. Categories include 1 to 2 times greater than the poverty line, 2 to 3 times greater than the poverty line, and more than 3 times the poverty line. These categories are entered as dummy variables in the logistic regression models and compared to poverty status youth (the reference category). The results are presented in Table A-22 for both

delinquency and drug use. The results for delinquency are presented in the left panel, and the results for drug use in the right panel.

As in previous sensitivity analyses, only symbols indicating statistical significance are presented. In Model 1, the coefficients for the interactions between all three poverty ratio dummy variables are positive and significant, indicating that delinquency is more strongly associated with dropout as the ratio of household income to the poverty line increases. (In fact, although coefficients are not shown in the table, the coefficient for the "3 times the poverty line" group is actually the largest of all the groups, indicating that delinquency is most strongly associated with dropout among the most well-off youth.) However, when observed controls are added in Model 2, all three interaction terms drop from significance. The results from the within-person interactions in Model 3 confirm the previous finding that the *descriptive* differences in delinquency between poor and non-poor do not translate into differences in *effects* for the two groups.

When looking at the results for drug use, in Model 1, the coefficients from the three interactions between drug use and the poverty ratio variables are positive and significant. As youth move farther away from the poverty line, drug use is more strongly associated with dropout. However, Models 2 and 3 reveal that this association is again not causal—when strong between-person controls are considered, drug use does lead to drop out, but there are no differences in effects for youth from different social classes.

The Role of Social Sanctions

<u>Do the effects of delinquency and drug use on dropout depend on whether a youth was sanctioned for the behavior?</u>
To answer this question, I reran the same three logistic regression models, this time including interactions between delinquency and school suspension and arrest, and between drug use and school suspension and arrest. In a second set of analyses, the models included three-way interactions between delinquency (or drug use) and school suspension (or arrest) and poverty status. This allows me to test whether any moderating effects of suspension and arrest differ by social class.

Table A-23 presents the results from the logistic regression models predicting dropout including two-way interactions between delinquency and suspension and arrest. In Model 1, the coefficient for the interaction between delinquency and school suspension is negative and significant. This indicates that youth who commit delinquency *and* are suspended are more likely to drop out. For a youth who commits one offense and is not suspended, the odds of dropout are 12.1 [(exp(.115)-1)*100] percent. For a youth who commits one offense and is suspended, the odds of dropout are 2.7 times (exp(.115+.928-.063) the odds for those who were not suspended. However, because the coefficient for the interaction between delinquency and suspension is negative, being suspended is less strongly associated with dropout for youth who are more heavily involved in delinquency, a finding which has been reported elsewhere (Sweeten 2006). This is not surprising, since the most delinquent youth are already at a high risk for dropout because of their behavior—being suspended from school is unlikely to change their likelihood of dropout. A similar result is obtained for arrest.

The interactions between delinquency and suspension/arrest are still significant in Model 2 when observed controls for selection are included, while the delinquency and arrest interaction drops from significance. However, in Model 3, the interaction of the within-person components for delinquency and suspension (and delinquency and arrest) is not different from zero, indicating no interaction between delinquency and suspension or between delinquency and arrest. Being suspended or arrested for delinquency does make a youth more likely to drop out, but not because they were sanctioned. Rather, it appears that youth who are the target of school discipline and police find themselves in that type of situation because of some other characteristics.

Table A-24 presents a similar set of analyses for drug use. Focusing on the within-person coefficients for the interactions between drug use and suspension and between drug use and arrest, we see no evidence that being suspended or arrested enhances the effects of drug use on dropout. However, the "main effect" of the within-person coefficient for drug use is significant, indicating that increases in drug use do lead to dropout, regardless of whether a youth was suspended or arrested. Increasing participation drug use by one behavior increases the odds of dropout 5.0 [(exp(.049)-1)*100] percent.

<u>Does being sanctioned enhance the effects of delinquency and drug use for youth from one social class but not from the other?</u>
To answer this question, Table A-25 presents the results from the same three logistic regression models predicting dropout from delinquency,

this time with three-way interactions among delinquency, suspension, and poverty status, as well as between delinquency, arrest, and poverty status. For ease of interpretation, I will turn my attention directly to Model 3, which is the random effects model. The interpretation of the "main effects" terms are somewhat more complicated when multiple interaction terms are included in the model. The coefficient for delinquency gives the effect of changes in delinquency for non-poor youth who were not suspended or arrested. The odds of a dropout for non-poor youth who increases delinquency by one offense are .99 times the odds of those who commit no delinquency. This coefficient is not statistically different from 0, indicating that delinquency has no effect on dropout for non-poor youth who were not suspended or arrested.

The coefficient for the two-way interaction between delinquency and arrest is positive and statistically significant, indicating that increases in delinquency do lead to dropout for non-poor youth who are arrested. For non-poor youth, committing one offense and being arrested increases the odds of dropout about 18 [(exp(-.005*1 +.097*1 + .074*1)-1)*100] percent. The positive coefficient for the interaction between delinquency and arrest indicates that the conditioning effect of arrest on delinquency is greater with greater increases in delinquency. For example, the odds increase 26.5 [(exp(-.005*2 +.097*1 + .074*2)-1)*100] percent for youth who committed 2 delinquent offenses and were arrested once. Therefore, delinquency does lead to dropout for non-poor youth who are arrested.

The within-person coefficient for the three-way interaction term between delinquency, arrest, and poverty status in Model 3 is negative and significant. The conditioning effect of arrest on the relationship between delinquency and dropout is less strong for poor youth than it is for non-poor youth. To get the odds for poor youth who committed delinquency and who were arrested, we have to combine the main effects for delinquency and arrest with the two-way interactions between delinquency and arrest, delinquency and poverty status, arrest and poverty status, and the three-way interaction among delinquency, arrest, and poverty status. For poor youth, committing one offense and being arrested increases the odds of dropout about 0.1 [(exp(-.005*1+.097*1 +.121*1 -.069*1)-1)*100] percent. This difference is not significant from 0. Being poor essentially cancels out the conditioning effect of arrest on the delinquency-dropout relationship. Again, this suggests that being arrested does not enhance the effects of delinquency on dropout for poor youth but only for non-poor youth.[17]

Figure 4-5 plots the predicted probability of dropout for each survey year by delinquency, arrest, and poverty status. These predicted probabilities are derived from the random effects model (Model 3) that includes the three-way interaction among delinquency, arrest, and poverty status. The figure shows that overall, poor youth have a higher predicted probability of dropout than non-poor youth. Within each social class, youth who engaged in delinquency and were arrested also have higher predicted probability of dropout than those who engaged in delinquency but were not arrested. The conditioning effect of social class on the interaction between delinquency and arrest is demonstrated by the distance between the arrested and not arrested lines within the poor and non-poor groups. For poor youth, the difference in the predicted probabilities of dropout between youth who arrested and youth who were not arrested is smaller than the difference for non-poor youth. This illustrates the finding from the random effects models that delinquency leads to dropout for non-poor youth who were arrested but not for poor youth who were arrested.

Figure 4-5. Predicted probability of dropout from hybrid random effects model, by delinquency, arrest, and poverty status

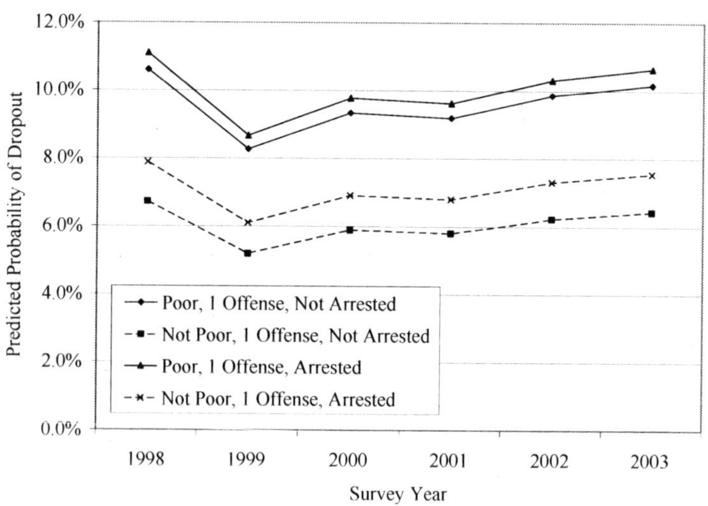

Table A-26 presents the results of models including an analogous set of interactions with drug use. As can be seen, in Model 3, none of the within-person coefficients for the interaction terms are significantly different from zero, indicating that suspension and arrest do not enhance the effects of drug use on dropout, regardless of social class.[18]

In sum, the results of this section indicate that delinquency does not always lead to dropping out. Specifically, it is important to take into account factors which might condition or enhance the effects of delinquency on dropping out, specifically, whether a youth is arrested and his or her social class background. Delinquency does lead to dropout for non-poor youth who are arrested, but not for poor youth, regardless of whether they are arrested. The negative effects of drug use on dropout do not seem to depend on whether a youth is suspended from school or arrested.[18]

CHAPTER 5

Toward a Theory of Precocious Development

While focus has shifted to the importance of a college degree for increasing the chances of attaining success in America, the high school diploma alone remains an important credential. In fact, the value of a high school diploma has never been greater. Over the past 25 years, earnings differences between high school graduates and high school dropouts have grown (Day and Newburger 2002). The rate of return to a high school diploma has increased to over 50 percent (Heckman, Lochner, and Todd 2008). Youth who miss out on this important developmental milestone are likely not only to find themselves without the skills to succeed in a competitive U.S. labor market that increasingly rewards skills and education but are also likely to be beset by other problems—including imprisonment, poor heath, and having children who are also at risk of high school dropout, to name a few. The costs of dropout and its associated ills fall not only on the individual dropout, but on the rest of society, as well. Indeed, it is estimated that the lifetime cost to the nation is $260,000 per dropout (Rouse 2005).

At the same time that the economic consequences of dropping out of high school have increased, Americans have been led to believe—vis-à-vis annual reports published by the U.S. Department of Education—that the high school graduation rate is over 90 percent (Barton 2005). However, in the past several years, reports by independent researchers have suggested a very different story: the U.S. is far from approaching universal high school completion. Only about two-thirds of youth are graduating from high school on time, and this number has been decreasing. Graduation rates for black and Hispanic youth are only about 50 percent. In this study, I have shown that dropping out of high school is not an uncommon experience for youth in the NLSY97, a nationally representative sample of U.S. youth; over 20 percent of youth drop out of high school at some point, and this figure is nearly double for youth from the most economically disadvantaged backgrounds.

Although several studies show that youth who engage in delinquency and drug use are more likely to drop out of high school, these studies provide little insight into *why* this is the case. While some studies have interpreted delinquency and drug use as causes of dropout, other studies find that problem behaviors are only weakly or not at all predictive of dropout once other factors associated with dropout are taken into consideration. This latter group of studies suggests that delinquency and drug use are symptoms of the underlying processes contributing to dropout in the first place.

This study contributed to existing literature on the effects of delinquency and drug use on dropout in three ways. First, I exploited the richness and panel design of the NLSY97 by using random effects models to estimate the effects of delinquency and drug use on dropout, which controlled for a wide array of observed as well as *unobserved* differences between youth. This strategy provided a more powerful test than prior studies of the claim that delinquency and drug use are causally related to dropout. Second, I explored whether getting into trouble at school or with the juvenile justice system amplifies the consequences of delinquency and drug use for dropout. Finally, I considered whether delinquency and drug use operate differently in the dropout process for middle-class and lower-class youth.

IMPLICATIONS FOR DELINQUENCY, DRUG USE, AND DROPOUT

Contribution of Delinquency and Drug Use to Dropout

My findings are more in line with studies that show that delinquency and drug use do not lead to dropout than with those that claim that delinquency and drug use cause dropout. When I included a wide array of observed control variables to capture differences between youth, the relationships between delinquency and dropout and between drug use and dropout were substantially attenuated. When I added controls for *unobserved* differences in the random effects model, the relationship between delinquency and dropout was eliminated and the relationship between drug use and dropout was reduced even further. Overall, being suspended from school or arrested did not enhance the consequences of delinquency and drug use. This finding suggests that the reason why youth who are involved in delinquency and drug use are also prone to dropout has *little or nothing to do* with their delinquency or drug use. Delinquency and drug use do not play major roles in putting youth on the path to dropout. However, because my approach was to control for *unobserved* differences between youth, the results do not reveal the underlying process that drives youth to engage in delinquency and drug use and to drop out. The next section proposes several possibilities for the underlying mechanism.

A Syndrome of Precocious Development

Earlier, I introduced two perspectives on why youth who are involved in delinquency and drug use are also prone to dropout—problem behavior theory (Jessor and Jessor 1977) and precocious development (Newcomb and Bentler 1988). Both perspectives view dropout as occurring not in isolation but rather with other behaviors, such as a dislike of school, academic difficulties, and deviant or adult behavior, all of which signal more fundamental problems in a youth's life. The key difference between these two perspectives is in the constellation of behaviors that comprise the "syndrome." Whereas the behaviors emphasized by the problem behavior perspective are considered deviant at all life stages, precocious development also includes prosocial adult behaviors, such as becoming a parent or working. A key distinction, then, is that problem behavior theory emphasizes a proneness to deviance as the motivation behind problem behavior, while precocious development focuses on the drive that many youth feel to be more independent and to gain adult status.

Neither a tendency toward deviance nor a drive to grow up quickly was measured directly in this study. Rather, I employed proxy variables for nonconventionality and precocious development that are manifestations of the presumed underlying problems but not direct measures of them. These included measures of school performance, deviant behavior other than delinquency and drug use, and adult role transitions. While poor school performance and sexual intercourse could be evidence of a syndrome of problem behavior or precocious development, adult role transitions like working more than 20 hours per week unambiguously captures precocious development. Introducing these measures substantially reduced but did not eliminate the relationships between delinquency and dropout and drug use and dropout. However, the additional random effects adjustments for unobserved selection factors completely eliminated the relationship between delinquency and dropout and further reduced the relationship between drug use and dropout. Given these findings, it appears that these unobserved selection factors capture more fundamental elements of the mechanisms that govern not only dropout, but also the proclivity to delinquency and drug use.

Although the underlying process driving youth to engage in delinquency and drug use and to drop out is unobserved in my models, the "syndrome" of observed behaviors that characterizes youth who participate in delinquency and drug use still has implications for these two explanations. Table A-27 provides a look at some of theses differences for delinquency. Table A-28 presents a similar analysis for drug use. Youth who engage in delinquency and drug use differ from those who do not on a wide variety of characteristics. Demographic factors, including race, household income, and parental education are only weakly associated with delinquency or drug use. Larger differences can be found in terms of school performance. Delinquents and drug users have lower GPAs in 8th grade and much higher rates of grade retention. Sexual intercourse is more strongly associated with delinquency and drug use than any other factor in Tables A-27 and A-28. The percentage of youth who are sexually active among the heaviest delinquents (more than six different offenses) is over five times as many as among non-delinquents. The heaviest drug users are six times as likely to have had sex as are non-users.

Although the connection of school failure and sexual intercourse with delinquency and drug use is reminiscent of a "syndrome" of problem behaviors, working more than 20 hours per week is also strongly related to delinquency and drug use. The percentage of youth who work more than 20 hours per week is more than twice as high among the heaviest delinquents compared to non-delinquents, and the heaviest drug users are three times as likely to work intensively as are non-users. This finding is more in line with precocious development theory as an explanation for delinquency, drug use, and dropout than with problem behavior theory, since problem behavior theory would not predict that working would be part of the constellation of behaviors.

This picture of youth who engage in delinquency and drug use aligns with Newcomb and Bentler's (1988) depiction of an adolescent drug use "lifestyle" that "includes rebellion, nonconformity to traditional values, involvement with other deviant or illegal behaviors and with individuals engaged in such behavior, poor family connections, few educational interests, precocious involvement in sexual activities, experiences of emotional turmoil, lack of social connection, alienation, and precocious involvement with the work force and earning money" (215).

Explaining Delinquency, Drug Use, and Dropout

A successful adolescence often requires delaying the rewards and social status that come with adulthood. Youth are required to stay in school until age 16. They cannot obtain a driver's license before age 16 or 17, drink alcohol before age 21, vote before age 18, or even have sex before age 18 in some jurisdictions. Most adolescents are financially dependent on their parents and do not have a say in important decisions that affect their lives. Yet many adolescents reach biological maturity earlier than age 16 and desire to start sexual relationships, to accrue materials possessions, to make decisions on their own, and to be afforded the status that comes with being an "adult." Many adolescents feel trapped in a gap between their biological and social ages. While wanting to escape this "maturity gap" is a normal part of adolescence, for some youth, the drive to transition to adult roles is more urgent. Precocious youth, according to Newcomb and Bentler (1988), evidence a "pseudomaturity," analogous to what Bachman (1983) has referred to as "premature affluence" and the Jessors' (1977) concept of "transition proneness". Such youth take on adult roles "without the necessary growth and development to enhance success" and "they will have a greater probability of failing at these roles over time" (36).

For such "precocious" youth, delinquency and drug use bridge this maturity gap, providing them with adult status, if only temporary. Some types of delinquency, such as property crimes, provide youth with possessions that are inaccessible to youth who are financially dependent on their parents, such as money to buy clothes, cars, cigarettes, or alcohol. Delinquency also gives youth the opportunity to "hang out" with older, more "mature" youth who are more experienced in committing delinquency and have successfully demonstrated that they are independent. Delinquency is also likely to lead to confrontations with a youth's parents and teachers, sending the message that he or she is "too old" to follow rules that are meant for younger youth. Smoking cigarettes and drinking alcohol, which are behaviors that are reserved for adults, provide youth with additional accoutrements of adulthood.

Given that precocious youth want to be more like adults, they are likely to find the youth-oriented environment of high school an unwelcoming place, one that is incompatible with their desire for more "grown up" activities. Being disinterested in school and to perform poorly weaken attachment to school, a problem compounded by grade retention, the strongest predictor of dropout identified in this study. Because of their academic difficulties and poor behavior, many precocious youth find themselves held back one or more grades. Being over-age for grade, precocious youth are surrounded by younger youth whose interests will surely seem "immature" to them, increasing their perception of a disjunction between their biological and social ages. Making matters worse, their on-time classmates are likely to see them as "dumb."

For youth who feel that school is too restrictive of their freedom and who are looked down upon at school because of their lack of academic success, the world outside may seem an attractive alternative to being in school. They may see starting an intimate relationship or getting a part-time job as a way of gaining independence, adult status, and possibly more satisfaction in the wider world than they are getting from school. For example, having sex gives youth the freedom to choose a partner (possibly one who is older or at least acts like it by having sex), to make their own decisions about their relationship, and to engage in a behavior that is clearly reserved for adults. Similarly, working at a job gives youth an opportunity to gain some degree of financial independence from parents and to engage in adult leisure activities with their older coworkers, such as smoking cigarettes or drinking alcohol, and possibly to feel better about themselves in a responsible role.

"Pseudomature" youth are likely to see dropping out of high school as the route to the more adult lifestyle that they desire. Youth who drop out are free from the childlike culture of high school, with all of its restrictions on their behavior and humiliation from failure. Dropouts can control their own time and are not bound by a class schedule. Dropouts can move out of their parents' residences and live on their own or with older friends. They can secure a job or transition to full-time employment if they already have a part-time job. Unlike other adult roles to which precocious youth may transition, such as employment, shedding the student role (or dropping out) is one generally looked down upon and for younger youth is often illegal, since society recognizes the importance of a high school diploma. The deviant status of dropout additionally evidences a willingness to break rules and to engage in behavior that puts their futures at risk. And like delinquency and drug use, dropping out is likely to create conflict with parents, an effect which employment may not have.

Delinquency and drug use fit into this picture as symptoms of a "syndrome" of precocious development, and not as causes of dropout. Such precocious youth are seduced by the short-lived experiences of adulthood afforded to them by delinquency, drug use, sexual relationships, and employment. Dropping out and the lifestyle surrounding it afford much the same inducements and gratifications. Such youth are likely to drop out of school, but not because of their delinquency and drug use. Delinquency, drug use, and dropout are indicative of a youth's desire to grow up quickly and transition to adulthood. Future research would be wise to seek out and include additional facets of precocious development not considered by this study, such as associations with older peers, or its root causes, such as the inability to delay gratification posited by Newcomb and Benter (1988).

Delinquency, Drug Use, and Precocious Development

Although delinquency, drug use, and dropout are manifestations of precocious development, drug use seems to play a slightly different role in dropout than delinquency. Unlike delinquency, drug use did lead to dropout when controls for unobserved selection factors were included. However, the effects were small and mostly concentrated among frequent users, suggesting that it is not drug use *per se* but rather frequent drug use that is consequential for dropout. These findings seem to accord with Friedman, Glickmand, and Utada's (1983) conclusion that "(w)hile drug use may not be the main cause of dropping out of high school, but only a concomitant effect of earlier, more fundamental state of disaffection from school, it is nevertheless clear that drug use by adolescents interferes with academic progress in high school" (353). The difference in effects of delinquency and drug use, although small, is not inconsequential and may provide a more nuanced understanding of how these behaviors are connected to dropout.

One possible explanation for why drug use, but not delinquency, leads to dropout is that drug use has physiological effects that interfere with academics independent of any underlying problems that led to drug use in the first place. Newcomb and Bentler (1988) claim that chronic drug use can have psychoactive effects on cognitive, affective, and behavioral processes, which may impair the ability to function in the role of student.   These effects on cognitive functioning are obviously not shared with delinquency. However, the sufficiency of this explanation is called into question by the fact that tobacco use— which would not be expected to impair cognitive functioning—had the largest effects of any drug on dropout.

A more plausible explanation is that delinquency and drug use have different meanings for youth in the context of precocious development. Drug use, which here includes smoking cigarettes and drinking alcohol, along with marijuana use, is "age-inappropriate" behavior for teens. Much of what constitutes delinquency, on the other hand (especially the more serious types of delinquency considered in this study), is socially inappropriate regardless of age. Because drug use is more closely tied to age norms and expectations than delinquency, it may more clearly signal adult status to the user and to other youth.   Newcomb and Bentler (1988) argue that the self-perception and perception by others of drug use as mature "propels that drug user into adult roles prematurely" (37). The "adultlikeness" of drug use relative to delinquency convinces a youth and others that he or she is ready to take on adult roles, such as employment or dropout. While both behaviors may be motivated by a strong drive to grow up quickly, drug use may be the more powerful impetus insofar as it more clearly imparts or signifies adult standing.

A second possibility is that youth who use drugs may be less prone to dropout *before* they start using drugs than youth who commit delinquency. Experimentation with drugs is a normal part of testing limits for many teens and may not always reflect the same "syndrome" of precocious development that is associated with delinquency. Indeed, drug use (which includes smoking cigarettes, drinking alcohol, and using marijuana) is more prevalent than delinquency among youth in the NLSY97—at least 84 percent of youth used drugs at some point between rounds 1 and 7. A youth's choice of delinquency over drug use may represent a more "extreme" way of coping with a prolonged adolescence and may represent a more advanced stage in the development of a "syndrome" of problem behaviors (Kandel 1989). Because it is more normative than delinquency, drug use may have greater potential to take youth "off track."

It may also follow that abstaining from drug use may be a protective factor against dropping out. Because drug use is wide spread among adolescents, youth who abstain from drug use may be different than the majority of youth in ways that make staying the course in school the likely outcome for them. For example, youth who are not smoking cigarettes or drinking alcohol may find more comfort in spending more "social" time with their parents, who can monitor their school performance and behavior, than at parties with other youth who are engaging in more "age-inappropriate" behavior. Abstainers may also go through puberty at an older age, which would make them less susceptible to the effects of a "maturity gap," and therefore less likely to use drugs and to drop out.

This study was unable to provide much insight into the specific mechanisms linking drug use to dropout. Getting suspended from school or arrested did not explain why drug use contributed to dropout. It may be important to consider a youth's relationships with his or her parents and peers. If parents discover that their teen is using drugs, they may become overly controlling, which could lead to a deterioration in the quality of the youth's relationship with them. If the youth feels that his or her freedom is being revoked by parents, they may be tempted to escalate their autonomy-seeking by hanging out with other drug using youth that parents would not approve of or by disengaging from school. Any of these factors could enhance precocious development and lead to dropout. Future research should explore these possibilities.

The Social Context of Delinquency, Drug Use, and Dropout

The dynamic of precocious development that seems to underlie delinquency, drug use, and dropout is highly contextualized and is likely to play out differently depending on a youth's social class. I found that middle-class dropouts were more involved in delinquency and drug use than were lower-class dropouts. One way to understand this difference is to focus on how the underlying processes that give rise to delinquency, drug use, dropout, and other premature transitions may differ for middle-class and lower-class youth. An important difference may have to do with the underlying motivations for taking on adult roles. Some youth from disadvantaged backgrounds go through a process of "adultification" in which they increasingly take on adult responsibilities in order to provide for the families (Burton 2007) or to provide companionship for a single parent. For example, a disadvantaged youth may have to care for a younger sibling because their family cannot afford day care or work at a part-time job after school to supplement a family's income. Such youth are not taking on adult responsibilities owing to a "maturity gap" but rather to help the family. Under such circumstances, there may not be a perceived disjuncture between their biological and social ages, with adult responsibilities thrust upon them.

While the reasons why middle-class youth make premature transitions are not well understood, they are likely to be very different. One may speculate that for middle-class youth, taking on adult roles may have more to do with feeling trapped in a "maturity gap." Because middle-class youth are better off economically, they are unlikely to have to help with family finances. Middle-class youth may be more likely to feel the effects of the paradoxes of adolescence. For example, living in the suburbs and not having a car may leave middle-class youth less able to have freedom to come and go as they please than if they lived in a city and had access to public transportation. Lacking the adult responsibilities that lower-class youth already have, middle-class youth may seek opportunities outside of school, like a part-time job, as a way of gaining independence and proving that they can conquer new challenges.

Dropping out of high school is unlikely to be a freely chosen decision for "adultified" lower-class youth who are challenged in balancing school with personal and financial responsibilities. Given that youth engage in delinquency and drug use because of the sampling of adult life they provide, it makes sense that lower-class dropouts, for whom quitting school more often follows from grown up responsibilities and probably is not discretionary, would be less prone to turn to problem behaviors as an outlet. Such youth do not need to engage in delinquency and drug use to experience what it is like to be an adult. By the same token, it is not surprising that delinquency and drug use would be more a part of the experience of dropout for middle-class youth, whose transition to adult roles is about gaining the very adult status that delinquency and drug use (and dropout) afford.

In addition to the reasons for premature transitions, contextual differences in the meaning of dropout for middle-class and lower-class youth may also be important. Leaving high school without a diploma is less "class appropriate" for middle-class than for lower-class youth. Because dropping out is less common among middle-class adolescents, we would expect it to be more strongly associated with other age-inappropriate behaviors, such as delinquency and drug use. In disadvantaged communities where dropping out is the rule as often as it is the exception, we would expect it to be less tied to delinquency and drug use.

Rather than focusing on the underlying processes that give rise to delinquency, drug use, and dropout, another way to explain differences in delinquency and drug use between middle-class and lower-class dropouts is to focus on the different consequences that these behaviors may have. I found that delinquency contributed to dropout for middle-class youth who were arrested. Delinquency did not contribute to dropout for lower-class youth, regardless of whether they were arrested. Because of their relatively advantaged economic position, most middle-class adolescents are likely to experience some degree of success in school and to have few demands on their time and energy from personal and financial responsibilities outside of school. Most middle-class youth are on track to graduate from high school. Because they have fewer other problems in their lives, an arrest. which violates norms of class-acceptable conduct, is more likely to stand out as a distinctive risk factor for dropout.

An arrest may mark the beginning of an accelerated transition to adulthood for middle-class youth who engage in delinquency as a way of expressing autonomy. Appearing in court and having an attorney, probation officer, or social worker may make a middle-class youth feel that he or she has real consequence in the adult world. Justice system processing is likely to expose middle-class youth to older, more hardened delinquents in the justice system or at school who may appear to have successfully "knifed off" childhood apron strings and demonstrated their independence. Such youth may serve as role models for a middle-class youth looking to shorten adolescence. Moreover, being arrested could lead teachers to see a middle-class youth as a troublemaker and strain relationships. In turn, middle-class youth may adopt a disrespect for the authority of school, and the acquisition of a delinquent "label" is likely to lead to a decided shift in his or her self-image, with "deviant" blending into "grown up." Youth who internalize this label may enact it by continued delinquency and other premature transitions, including dropping out of school.

This dynamic plays out very differently at the other end of the socioeconomic spectrum. Many lower-class youth lack the economic, family, and personal resources that make graduating from high school probable. Often, they experience little academic success and many are immersed in competing responsibilities outside of school. The odds of graduating from high school are stacked against lower-class adolescents. Given that graduating from high school is uncertain for lower-class adolescents to begin with, there is little room for arrest to make a distinctive difference: with multiple, powerful forces already at play, the additional impetus of an arrest is not needed for them to quit school. Such youth are at risk for drop out whether or not they are arrested. Moreover, a delinquent "label" is unlikely to change lower-class youths' self-image or the way that teachers treat them, since lower-class youth may already be considered poor prospects. For lower-class youth, an arrest appears to be just one more experience among many in an accelerated transition to adulthood. This finding is consistent with Hannon's (2003) disadvantage saturation perspective, which argues that deviant behavior and arrest have consequences for the educational attainment of middle-class but not lower-class youth.

IMPLICATIONS FOR THE DROPOUT PROCESS

Causes of Dropout

If delinquency and drug use are not the main causes of dropout, what are? Identifying the causes of dropout is by no means an easy task since many of the factors associated with dropout, such as delinquency and drug use, are symptoms of underlying problems rather than causes dropout (Rumberger 1987). For the most part, my findings are not surprising and largely in agreement with the existing literature on dropout. The "profile" of a dropout identified in this study is one of a youth who is leaving the student role, entering adult roles ahead of the socially perceived timetable, and engaging in delinquency and drug use. School problems and adult role transitions are the two features of the "profile" that have the greatest consequences for dropout. Grade retention had stronger effects than any other factor on dropout. The consequences of grade retention for dropout are well documented (Alexander et al. 2001; Jimerson, Anderson, and Whipple 2002). Also consistent with the literature (Rumberger and Larson 1998; Swanson and Schneider 1999), school mobility had an effect on dropout.

Adult role transitions also play a critical role. Sexual intercourse, a factor which is surprisingly absent in studies of dropout, had a strong effect (but see Frisco 2008; Mensch and Kandel 1988). Since the effect of childbearing was controlled, the effect of sexual intercourse on dropout was not due to the unintended consequence of having a baby. Rather, starting sexual relationships may distract from academic pursuits by focusing a youths' mental energy on the relationship and away from schoolwork (Schneider and Stevenson 1999) or by reducing parental supervision.

Intensive employment (working more than 20 hours per week) also led to dropout. This finding is at odds with recent indications in the literature that employment may not be as harmful to youth as originally assumed (Paternoster et al. 2003; Shanahan and Flaherty 2001; Warren 2002), although for some youth under some circumstances employment may be harmful (Staff and Lee 2007). The reason for this finding is unclear, but one possibility is that this study did not consider some potentially dynamic factor that might cause both adolescent employment and dropout, such as association with delinquent peers. Nevertheless, the findings for adult role transitions suggest that sexual intercourse and intensive employment are not just symptoms of a lack of success in the student role: a taste of the adult status that comes with such premature transitions may increase a youth's appetite for more independence and lead to dropout.

It is important to note that while my primary interest was in the effects of delinquency, drug use, and other individual behaviors on dropout, dropout is not an individual problem. Rather, the root causes of dropout are structural in nature. I documented large differences in dropout rates across social lines, including social class and race. It is interesting to point out that socioeconomic status (measured by household income and parental education) continued to exert a strong effect on dropout, even with other controls included, suggesting that socioeconomic status influences dropout independent of school failure, premature transitions, and problem behaviors. One possibility is that the quality of schooling, which was not considered in this study, further explains why socioeconomic status is still linked to dropout. Future research should investigate the "unexplained variance" in the socioeconomic status-dropout link.

A Long-Term Developmental View of Dropout

A second implication of this study for our understanding of dropout is that quitting school (and the constellation of problem and precocious behaviors that often accompanies it) is a long-term developmental process. A life course perspective views dropout as a long-term *process* of disengagement from school rather than an *event* (1997; Alexander et al. 2001). Several studies have shown that school performance and behavior as early as first grade distinguish future dropouts from future graduates (Alexander et al. 1997; Alexander et al. 2001; Cairns et al. 1989; Ensminger and Slusarcick 1992). The finding that taking on delinquency and drug use in adolescence does not alter youths' chances of graduating suggests that the causes of delinquency, drug use, and dropout predate adolescence, a conclusion which resonates with a life course view of dropout as a long-term process. By adolescence, the dynamic that gives rise to dropout (and to delinquency and drug use) is well established.

Exactly what does this dynamic look like? Unfortunately, the truncated nature of the NLSY97 data does not allow me to fully view this process. Because even the youngest NLSY97 youth were age 12 when they first interviewed, much of the development process underlying dropout occurred before the survey began. Nevertheless, the data do provide some limited insight into this dynamic. Demographic background, including socioeconomic status (as measured by household income and parental education) and mother's age at the youth's birth were highly predictive of dropout. This suggests that factors from early childhood can affect whether youth eventually drop out or graduate.

Demographic factors are likely to have an effect on early school performance. School failure launches many youth into a cycle of disengagement similar to that described by Finn's (1989) frustration-self-esteem and participation-identification models of dropout. Lack of success in the student role can lead to delinquency and drug use as a way of recouping self-esteem. Problem behaviors may create confrontations with school officials and parents, fueling the process of failure and disengagement. Youth who get off to a bad start in school are likely to find themselves trapped in a cycle of adaptation to failure that involves disengagement and problem behavior leading to dropout. In contrast, for youth who get off to a good start, academic success reinforces continued engagement and prosocial behavior.

This dynamic process coalesces into a relatively stable pattern of academic failure, delinquency, and drug use that is well established by adolescence. When looking at a cross-sectional snapshot like the one provided by the NLSY97, this relatively stable pattern will resemble a "syndrome" of precocious development. By the time the NLSY97 catches up with youth, the process leading to problem behavior and dropout is well along for many eventual dropouts early in childhood. While delinquency and drug use may have played a role in the earlier process of leading to disengagement, given that dropout was so long in the making, in the near term they are more concomitant to dropout than impetus.

While patterns leading to dropout are likely to be established early in life, dropout is by no means set in stone by preadolescent processes. This study demonstrates that what happens later in life can also be critical. For youth who find little comfort at school and that the short-lived adult status provided by delinquency and drug use is no longer enough, "real" adult roles outside of school may seem like a more promising solution. However, succumbing to the lures of sexual relationships and employment increases their chances of leaving school, independently of the long-term process that set their "syndrome" of precocious development in motion. Such premature transitions may exacerbate the problems that led youth to be disengaged from school in the first place. Even for a youth who is disengaged from school, holding down a part-time job, for example, may further interfere with academic achievement by taking up their time and energy. Moreover, the tastes of adult status afforded by a job may confirm to a youth that he or she is better off dropping out and working full-time than staying in school.

Limitations and Future Research

This study has several limitations that should be addressed by future research. First, this study provides only a speculative explanation of the underlying processes that lead to delinquency, drug use, and dropout. Future researchers can better understand this process in two ways. First, the unobserved differences between youth that drive delinquency, drug use, and dropout should be identified. Since my statistical approach addressed selection on stable, individual differences, focusing on processes that predate adolescence is likely to be fruitful. Second, the possibility that drug use and dropout can be explained by processes not considered in this study should be explored. Changes in youths' lives that may predispose them to drug use and dropout other than those that were explicitly modeled could not be considered. One important factor that was not included is family processes. For example, parents who are uninvolved, frequently fight, or regularly change partners are likely to predispose youth to both drug use and dropout. If these aspects of family processes turn out to play a large role as an impetus to drug use and dropout, then the effects of drug use are overstated.

A second limitation of this study is that it was unable to shed much light on the reasons why delinquency leads to dropout for middle-class youth who are arrested and why drug use leads to dropout. There is a need to better understand what it is about being arrested that enhances the consequences of delinquency for middle-class youth. Possible explanations include time away from school, a shifting self-image, association with other delinquent youth, or differential treatment from teachers, school officials, or parents. Moreover, studies may wish to consider other factors that link drug use to dropout. The effects of drug use on school performance, motivation to succeed in school, and friendship groups would be productive places to start.

Finally, little is known about the possible cumulative, long-term effects of delinquency and drug use on dropout. This study employed a measure of delinquency in the past year and drug use in the past month predicting dropout, and thus assesses only the short-term effects of delinquency and drug use. However, it is possible that for youth who start offending at an early age and who continue to offend, short-term changes may be irrelevant to their dropout prospects. In fact, life course theories of delinquency (Moffitt 1993; Thornberry and Krohn 2001) suggest that delinquency and drug use would actually have long-term effects on dropout since the consequences of the behaviors require time to "snowball." Unfortunately, the truncated nature of the NLSY97 data set does not allow me to examine this possibility. The youngest cohort of youth are age 12 at round 1, and over half of respondents had reported already having engaged in at least one form of delinquency. For persistently delinquent youth, the connection between their behavior and dropout may well represent a causal process that began years before, which is not captured by this study. Future research should investigate the possible importance of early delinquency or drug use for dropout.

Implications for Policy

Recent dropout statistics have attracted a great deal of attention to dropout, including a story on the cover of *Time* magazine (Thornburgh 2006). Understanding how to prevent dropout is important due to the costs of dropout to the individual and to society. In 2006, the Gates Foundation released *The Silent Epidemic*, a study on high school dropout made several policy recommendations for preventing dropout (Bridgeland, DiIulio, and Morison 2006). One of those recommendations was to increase the age of compulsory school attendance. This study suggests that raising the age of compulsory school attendance without providing the necessary resources for academic success and making school more relevant to youths' lives may have the unintended consequences of increasing delinquency and drug use. Youth engage in delinquency and drug use (and drop out) because they are stigmatized by failure at school and want desperately to gain adult status. Prolonging youths' time in such an environment without providing some alternative means for success is likely to lead to increased delinquency and drug use.

This study has several other implications for dropout prevention. First, because delinquency and drug use are not the main causes of dropout, dropout prevention programs would be most effective when they focus their attention not on problem behaviors but rather recognize that a diverse array of academic and behavioral problems are associated not just with dropout, but also with delinquency and drug use. Dropout prevention programs may get more leverage by focusing on boosting academic performance, delaying the onset of sexual intercourse, and limiting the number of hours that youth can work during the school year. However, dropout will not be eliminated unless the structural causes that give rise to school failure and the need to take on adult-type responsibilities is addressed, such as the socioeconomic disparities that contribute to early setbacks in school. Addressing such issues will not be an easy task.

In the meantime, efforts to reduce dropout should focus on making high school a more welcoming place to youth with more adult lifestyles and interests. Many high school dropouts who smoke cigarettes, drink alcohol, have children, and work choose to finish high school by taking and passing a GED exam (Chuang 1997; Mensch and Kandel 1988; Obot and Anthony 2000). Many of these dropouts do not lack the motivation or ability to finish high school (Entwisle, Alexander, and Olson 2004) but find the GED more compatible with their lifestyles. But while the GED may provide such youth with a quicker, easier route out of high school, it is unlikely to provide them with the same financial rewards as a high school diploma (Cameron and Heckman 1993). Currently, there are no good alternatives to the four-year high school experience. While it is hard to imagine what such an alternative may look like, schools may want to consider providing youth with designated areas to smoke, day care, and opportunities to combine academics with real world work experience in order to better accommodate their interests and responsibilities outside school.

Third, most dropout prevention programs target youth in middle and high school. Since delinquency, drug use, and dropout have their roots in childhood, programs that start in adolescence are likely to be ineffective in breaking the well-established pattern of disengagement and problem behavior as well as costly. On the other hand, school engagement strategies that start in childhood could well help prevent youth from developing adaptations to school failure that involve problem behaviors and eventually culminate in dropout.

Finally, this study has implications for school disciplinary policies. In the wake of a series of school shootings in 1990s, school safety has become a priority. Many schools have adopted zero tolerance and other "get tough" policies in an effort to prevent school violence. Many schools have hired police officers (also known as "school resources officers" or SROs) to patrol the halls and enforce school rules. This practice has come under fire by critics who argue that minor infractions of school rules that would normally be handled by school officials are handled instead by law enforcement, which sometimes results in further involvement with the justice system and the "criminalization" of trivial offenses (Beger 2002; Dohrn 2001). Even more troubling is the fact that disadvantaged youth are overrepresented in school discipline (Skiba et al. 1997; Wu et al. 1982)

This study suggests that it is middle-class youth are most likely to be adversely affected by the use of police officers in schools. A youthful indiscretion that leads to an arrest by a school police officer could have the unintended result of foreclosing educational opportunity for a youth who is otherwise on the path to graduate from high school. Schools may wish to consider alternatives to police officers for enforcing school rules. Moreover, programs that divert middle-class youth away from the juvenile justice system may be effective in reducing middle-class dropout.

Conclusion

This study was motivated by the fact that for the majority of dropouts, involvement in delinquency and drug use seem to be an inescapable part of their high school experience, but that prior studies have often disagreed about whether delinquency and drug use lead to dropout. My main finding is that the relationship among delinquency, drug use, and dropout is more complicated than prior studies have appreciated. First, there is a great deal of self-selection into delinquency and drug use as well as into dropping out. However, despite these shared causes, there are some situations in which delinquency and drug use do lead to dropout, although the effects are small. Specifically, delinquency leads to dropout for middle-class youth who are arrested, and drug use leads to dropout for middle- and lower-class youth alike. Nevertheless, for the most part, I conclude that it is mainly other underlying causes that prompt all three behaviors: delinquency, drug use, and dropout.

Future research would be well-advised to pursue three different lines of inquiry. First, future research should focus on identifying the underlying mechanisms that lead youth to get involved in delinquency and drug use and ultimately to drop out of high school. Identifying these processes would lead to a better understanding of why youth drop out of school, and in particular, why youth who participate in delinquency and drug use drop out of school. It would also facilitate identification of much more consequential influences on dropout than delinquency or drug use. Second, research should continue to pay attention to the differences between varieties of dropout, as multiple dropout processes may be at work for different groups of youth. Little research to date has examined these issues. Third, future research would be well adivsed to consider the mechansims that link delinquency to dropout for middle-class youth and drug use to dropping out for both groups. While it may be difficult to prevent youth from experimenting with delinquency or drug use, by understanding the mediating variables in the delinquency-dropout and drug use-dropout relationships, it may be possible to moderate, if not eliminate, their consequences for dropout. Finally, future research would be wise to consider the heterogeneity of dropouts in ways other than social class—including dropouts' reasons for leaving school—or the heterogeneity of delinquents—such as age of onset. Only through further inquiry will we fully understand why problem behavior-prone youth are also on the path to dropout. This study represents a first attempt at that.

Endnotes

1. Christopher Swanson and Duncan Chaplin used data from the Common Core of Data (CCD) to calculate the Cumulative Promotion Index (CPI). The value of the CPI approximates the probability that a student entering ninth grade will complete high school four years later with a regular diploma. They find a national graduation rate of 66.6 percent. They also observed dramatic racial disparities in high school completion, with white and Asian students graduating at much higher rates than students from historically disadvantaged minority groups. White and Asian students complete high school at 75 and 77 percent, respectively. By contrast, graduation rates for black and Hispanic students are 50 and 53 percent, respectively.

2. Not all of the round 1 interviews were conducted in 1997. Most of the round 1 interviews occurred between January 1997 and October 1997. However, due to concerns over the number of age-eligible youth found during the initial fielding period, NLSY97 staff interviewed at additional 395 respondents during a refielding period between March 1998 and May 1998.

3. The procedure for obtaining a youth's enrollment status was somewhat more complicated in round 1 than in later rounds due to the refielding period. As previously mentioned, round 1 interviews extended into the summer of 1997, when many youth were not enrolled in school because they were on summer vacation. Youth who reported not being enrolled were asked an additional series of questions to determine whether their non-enrollment was due to being a dropout or because they were on summer vacation. Youth who were on summer vacation reported whether they were enrolled in summer school and when the last time was that they were enrolled. Respondents who were enrolled at the time of the survey, those on break who reported being enrolled in the spring of 1997, and those who were in summer school and reported being enrolled during the 1996-97 academic school year were classified as enrolled. All other respondents were classified as not being enrolled (e.g., interviewed during the school year and

not enrolled, on break and not enrolled in the spring of 1997, in summer school and not enrolled during the 1996-97 academic year).

4. The reference period for vandalism, petty theft, major theft, other property crimes, aggravated assault, and selling drugs in 1997 is the past year. The reference period for all other offenses is since birth.

5. The NLSY97 also queries respondents on their use of hard drugs, including cocaine and LSD. Unfortunately, for reasons unknown to me, this question was not asked in 1997. Therefore, the measure of drug use employed here omits this measure. However, since hard drug use may have greater effects on dropout, supplementary analyses were conducted that included the measure of hard drug use in the years in which it was available. These results are discussed in the next chapter.

6. The SAQ does solicit information from respondents on their frequency of participation in some of the delinquent offenses and drug use behaviors. Information on past year frequency is available for vandalism, petty theft, major theft, other property crimes, aggravated assault, and selling drugs. Past month frequency is available for carrying a handgun. For drug use, past month frequency is available for cigarette smoking, alcohol use, marijuana use, binge drinking, and using alcohol and marijuana before or during school or work. Additional sensitivity analyses are presented in the results section that employ frequency measures of delinquency and drug use constructed from the available items.

7. However, as Jarjoura (1996) notes, it is important to examine differences within the non-poverty group, since this group is quite large. Not all youth whose household income is above the poverty line should be considered "middle-class." Several alternative measures of social class have been constructed and sensitivity analyses conducted. Results will be presented in the next chapter.

8. In round 1, there is no question asking whether youth were arrested in the past year. Instead, youth are asked whether they have ever been arrested and, if so, the month and year of their first arrest and most recent arrest. Using these dates, I constructed a variable indicating whether the youth had been arrested in the year preceding the 1997 interview.

9. There is some ambiguity surrounding the nature of the relationship between socioeconomic status (SES) and delinquency. Early studies based on official police records showed that social class was inversely related to arrest and police contact (Braithwaite 1981; Tracy 1990). Early self-report studies, however, told a somewhat different story, namely, that there was a

weak or non-existent relationship between social class and delinquency (Tittle, Villemez, and Smith 1978). More recent studies (Elliott and Huizinga 1983; Elliott, Huizinga, and Ageton 1985) suggest that social class is unrelated to minor delinquency but that lower class youth commit a disproportionate share of serious delinquency. In the NLSY97, I have found that SES was unrelated to delinquency but positively associated with drug use. The latter is not surprising, given that the items included in the substance use measure are relatively minor (e.g., smoking, drinking, using pot). Nevertheless, because SES is clearly related to dropout, and because my primary goal is to address selection, I err on the side of caution and control for SES.

10. Household income changes over time and could be treated as a time-varying covariate. Household income is measured not only in round 1 of the NLSY97 but also at every later round to date. However, the amount of missing data on this variable increases substantially in later rounds.

11. A second issue that must be addressed before drawing inferences from the data is the clustered nature of the NLSY97 sample. There are two levels of clustering in the NLSY97. First, the multistage stratified sampling design selected respondents in certain PSUs or geographic regions. Respondents in the same region would be expected to be more similar to each other than respondents in different regions. The second level of clusting is at the household level. In the NLSY97, 3,855 respondents are siblings, making it extremely important to correct for household clustering. Since SAS cannot correct for clustering at more than one level, this study corrects for clustering only at the household level since design effects at that level would be expected to be greater than those associated with georgraphic region.

12. Weighted dropout rates will be representative of the population insofar as the analysis sample does not differ from the full sample.

13. Hard drug use was not included in the analyses because the annual measures of hard drug use were not available until 1999. The NLSY97 contains three variables tapping a youth's use of hard drugs, including cocaine, LSD, and prescription drug abuse: (1) prevalence of use in the past year, (2) frequency of use in the past year, and (3) frequency of use before or during school or work in the past year. While these variables were not available until 1999, I included these variables in a separate set of analyses designed to test the sensitivity of the findings to their inclusion. Inclusion of these additional measures in the drug use variety and frequency scales

did not change the magnitude of the effects of drug use on dropout. Moreover, when included separately, use of hard drugs had no effect on dropout.

14. Findings from this analysis should be interpreted with caution. This is because the use of increasingly longer lags necessitates the exclusion of younger person-year observations and youth from the sample. Since information on the variety and frequency of delinquency and drug use is not available for periods before round 1, the use of a three year lag requires that the first year in which dropout can be predicted is 2000 (by delinquency and drug use in 1999, 1998, and 1997). Information on dropout from 1997, 1998, and 1999 has to be discarded. This has the effect of ignoring information on dropout that occurs at younger ages, even though such information is available. For example, if a youth entered the sample at age 13, dropout before age 16 is ignored. For youth who entered the sample when they were 14 years old, information on dropout before age 17 is ignored, and so forth. While most dropout in the NLSY97 occurs at age 16 or later, results from models that use a three year time lag can only be thought of as generalizable to later dropout. Moreover, since the sample for these models is not just restricted to youth who have at least three person-year observations but rather to youth who have three person-year observations after 2000, significantly larger numbers of youth are lost due to sample attrition. The included youth are therefore not representative of all dropouts.

15. One reason for the difference between the findings for drug use variety and drug use frequency may have to do with variation in the measures and multicolinearity. The three lagged measures of drug use (or delinquency) are highly correlated. However, the variety scales are more highly correlated than are the frequency scales because they have a smaller range and less variability. To allow for this possibility, I reran all of the models with each of the lagged delinquency and drug use measures included separately rather than simultaneously, and the results obtained for frequency were replicated for variety.

16. I also ran models in which the dependent variable is the alternative measure of dropout. Recall that his measure does not count GED holders as dropouts but rather as graduates. This model is designed to test the sensitivity of the findings to how GEDs are treated, since prior research has revealed that GED holders have higher levels of drug use than graduates. The coefficients for delinquency and drug use (as well as the other variables) were very similar in magnitude to those in prior analyses.

17. Rather than dealing with multiple two- and three-way interaction terms, I reran Model 3 with the poverty status variable reverse coded, such that poor youth were coded as 0 and non-poor youth were coded as 1. The coefficient for the interaction gives the interaction between delinquency and arrest for poor youth (because poor is coded 0). This interaction terms was not significantly different from zero and the odds of dropout for poor youth who were arrested was similar to that obtained above. Similar results were obtained also by splitting the sample by poverty status.

18. Since black and Hispanic youth are overrepresented in the poverty sample, and since black and Hispanic youth also tend to underreport their delinquency, I examined whether the effects of delinquency and arrest on non-poor youth were being driven by poor black and Hispanic youth underreporting delinquency. To do this, I reran the models including interactions between poverty status and race. The results for black and Hispanic youth were not substantially different from those of white youth.

Appendix: Tables

Table A-1. Summary of prior studies on delinquency, drug use, and dropout

Study	Data and Sample	Delinquency/Drug Use Measure	Dropout Measure	Delinquency/Drug Use Predict Dropout?
Bachman et al. (2008)	Monitoring the Future	Drug use: frequency of daily smoking, past month alcohol use, past 2 weeks binge drinking, past month marijuana use, and past year cocaine use	No high school diploma or GED by age 22	Drug Use: Varied by drug type Cigarettes: Yes Alcohol: No Marijuana: No Cocaine: No
Ellickson et al. (1998)	RAND Adolescent Panel Study	Drug Use: Frequency of cigarette, alcohol, and marijuana use during 7th grade	Not enrolled in school and high school diploma or GED	Drug Use: Varied by drug type Cigarettes: Yes Alcohol: No Marijuana: No Cocaine: No
Fagan and Pabon (1990)	Adolescents from six inner city neighborhoods Multistage sample of 200 students in	Delinquency: Frequency and severity index for past 12 months of offenses ranging from petty offenses	Identified through chain referral methods of local social service agencies, community service	Delinquency: No Drug Use: No

Table A-1. Summary of prior studies on delinquency, drug use, and dropout (continued)

Study	Data and Sample	Delinquency/Drug Use Measure	Dropout Measure	Delinquency/Drug Use Predict Dropout?
	each neighborhood and purposive sample of 50 dropouts in each neighborhood	(e.g., going to school high or drunk) to index felonies Drug use: Frequency and severity in past 12 months	organizations, and other dropouts	
Friedman, Glickmand, and Utada (1983)	Students from two public urban high schools in Philadelphia 598 students who were in 9th, 10th, and 11th grade during the	Drug and alcohol problems scale, reflecting negative personal and social consequences of alcohol or drug use Drug use: "Drug Severity Index" derived from a formula which weighted and summed the following factors for 11 drugs: (1) the	N/A	Drug Use: Yes, but effects substantially reduced by inclusion of 21 demographic, family, and individual controls

Table A-1. Summary of prior studies on delinquency, drug use, and dropout (continued)

Study	Data and Sample	Delinquency/Drug Use Measure	Dropout Measure	Delinquency/Drug Use Predict Dropout?
	1980-1981 academic year	frequency of use during the preceding three months, (2) the "peak" frequency of past use, and (3) the number of years used and the "risk level" of the drug Amount of increase or decrease that occurred in the frequency and risk level of drug use during 8 months		
Janosz and LeBlanc (1998)	Longitudinal sample of 797 White and French-speaking adolescents from the city of Montreal (grades 7 through 9)	Delinquency: 21 item scale measuring participation in fighting, minor and major thefts, and vandalism in the past	Have not completed the minimal requirements for a secondary school level diploma by the age of 22, identified	Delinquency: Yes, but only for "maladjusted" dropouts—not for "quiet" dropouts Drug Use: Same

Table A-1. Summary of prior studies on delinquency, drug use, and dropout (continued)

Study	Data and Sample	Delinquency/Drug Use Measure	Dropout Measure	Delinquency/Drug Use Predict Dropout?
	who were interviewed in 1985 791 subjects (367 boys and 424 girls)	twelve months Drug use: 5 item scale measuring the frequency of use of alcohol, marijuana, and hard drugs in the past twelve months	using the national data set of the Department of Education of Quebec Distinguished maladjusted, quiet, and disengaged types	
Kaplan and Liu (1994)	Panel of 9,335 students in 36 randomly selected junior-senior high schools containing grade 7 in the Houston Independent School District in 1971 2,805 students who	Deviance: Variety of 14 items, including participation in gang fights, carrying a weapon starting a fight, and stealing objects worth less and $2 Drug use: Variety of marijuana and	Self-report of whether the student graduated from high school by the third wave	Drug Use: No once adult role transitions were included

Table A-1. Summary of prior studies on delinquency, drug use, and dropout (continued)

Study	Data and Sample	Delinquency/Drug Use Measure	Dropout Measure	Delinquency/Drug Use Predict Dropout?
	provided were present for all three testing occasions and who had complete data for all variables in the analysis	narcotics in the month preceding survey		
Krohn, Lizotte, and Perez (1995)	Rochester Youth Development Study (RYDS) 867 adolescents with complete data for waves 2-7 interviews Waves were spaced six months apart At wave 2, students were in the fall	Delinquency: Frequency of 44 serious delinquent acts (e.g., theft over $50, carrying a weapon, attack with a weapon, rape) in the 6 months across waves 2 and 3 Drug use: Frequency of use of 10 drugs across waves 2 and 3 (not including	Self-report of dropping out any time between waves 4 and 6 and having not return to school by Wave 6	Delinquency: No Drug Use: Yes

Table A-1. Summary of prior studies on delinquency, drug use, and dropout (continued)

Study	Data and Sample	Delinquency/Drug Use Measure	Dropout Measure	Delinquency/Drug Use Predict Dropout?
	semester of 8th or 9th grade	alcohol)		
Mensch and Kandel (1988)	At wave 7, students were in the spring semester of 10th or 11th grade NLSY79 6,062 males and 6,009 females who were interviewed in 1984 when they were aged 19-27	Delinquency: Frequency of 17 non-drug delinquent acts in the past year reported in 1980 Drug use: Ever prevalence and age of onset of tobacco use, alcohol use, marijuana use, and other illicit drug use (including cocaine and LSD)	Not enrolled at the date of any interview GEDs counted separately	Delinquency: Yes Drug Use: Yes

Table A-1. Summary of prior studies on delinquency, drug use, and dropout (continued)

Study	Data and Sample	Delinquency/Drug Use Measure	Dropout Measure	Delinquency/Drug Use Predict Dropout?
McCluskey, Krohn, Lizotte, and Rodriguez (2002)	Rochester Youth Development Study (RYDS) Waves 1 through 10	Frequency of illegal drug use in waves 1 through 5 (including alcohol, marijuana and hard drugs)	Self-reported dropout at wave 10 (age 20) Students not allowed to drop out before wave 6 (age 16)	Drug use: No for Latino males once impregnation was controlled, yes for white and black males

Table A-2. Controls included by prior studies

Variable	(1)	(2)	(3)	(4)	(5)	(6)	(7)	(8)	(9)	No. of Studies
Demographic										
SES		*	*	*	*	*	*	*	*	8
Race or Ethnicity		*		*	*	*			*	5
Gender	*	*	*	*	*	*		*		7
Age		*				*		*		3
Family Structure		*			*	*	*	*	*	6
Urbanicity						*			*	2
School										
Academic Achievement			*					*	*	3
Grade Retention	*	*			*		*	*	*	6
Involvement		*		*	*					3
Commitment to School					*					1
Educational						*		*	*	3
Expectations										
Intelligence					*					1
Parents' Expectations					*					1
Parents' Involvement					*			*		2
Family	*	*			*					3
Attachment to Parents	*				*		*	*		4
Parental Supervision	*									1

Table A-2. Controls included by prior studies (continued)

Variable	(1)	(2)	(3)	(4)	(5)	(6)	(7)	(8)	(9)	No. of Studies
Neighborhood Violence	*									1
School Crime	*									1
Peer Delinquency	*						*	*	*	4
Victim Status	*									1
Adult Role Transitions	*			*		*	*		*	5
Conventional Values		*				*				2
Religious Affiliation		*		*						2
Psychological Distress						*				1
Self-esteem						*			*	2
Locus of Control				*						1
Self-control				*						1

Note: (1) Fagan and Pabon (1990), (2) Friedman, Glickmand, and Utada (1983), (3) Janosz and LeBlanc (1998), (4) Kaplan and Liu (1994), (5) Krohn, Lizotte, and Perez (1995), (6) Mensch and Kandel (1988), (7) McCluskey, Krohn, Lizotte, and Rodriguez (2002), (8) Ellickson et al. (1998), and (9) Bachman et al. (2008)

Table A-3. Variable definitions

Variable	Definition
Dropout	
Dropout	=1 if youth is not enrolled in high school and does not have a diploma (GED holders are counted as dropouts)
Dropout (alternative definition)	=1 if youth is not enrolled in high school and does not have a diploma or GED
Delinquency and Drug Use	
Delinquency	Variety of involvement in 21 different offenses since last interview (or ever in round 1): (1) carrying a handgun, (2) vandalism, (3) petty theft, (4) petty shoplifting, (5) petty larceny, (6) petty burglary, (7) petty armed robbery, (8) major theft, (9) major shoplifting, (10) major larceny, (11) major burglary, (12) major armed robbery, (13) vehicle theft, (14) receiving income from stolen property, (15) "other" property crimes (including possessing or receiving stolen property), (16) income from "other" property crime, (17) aggravated assault, (18) selling illegal drugs, (19) selling marijuana, (20) selling hard drugs, and (21) income from selling drugs
Drug Use	Variety of involvement in 7 different drug use activities in the 30 days preceding the interview: (1) smoking cigarettes, (2) smoking more than one pack of cigarettes per day, (3) drinking alcohol, (4) binge drinking (defined as 5 or more drinks on one occasion), (5) drinking alcohol

Table A-3.   Variable definitions (continued)

Variable	Definition
	before or during school or work, (6) using marijuana, and (7) using marijuana before or during school or work
Social Class	
Poverty Status	=1 if youth's household was below the poverty line in 1996
Social Sanctions	
Suspended from School	=1 if youth was suspended from school since the last interview
Arrested	=1 if youth was arrested since the last interview
Control Variables	
Demographics	
Age	Youth's age (in years)
Gender	
Female (ref. category)	=1 if youth is female
Male	=1 if youth is male
Race	
White (ref. category)	=1 if youth is white
Black	=1 if youth is black
Hispanic	=1 if youth is Hispanic

Table A-3. Variable definitions (continued)

Variable	Definition
Asian	=1 if youth is Asian
Other Race	=1 if youth is other race
Parental Education	Highest grade completed by either residential parent
1996 Household Income (Log)	Youth's household income in 1996 (natural log)
Mother < 20 at Birth	=1 if youth's mother was 19 years old or younger when she gave birth to the youth
Family Structure	
Both Biological Parents (ref. category)	=1 if youth lives with both biological parents
Biological Mother Only	=1 if youth lives with biological mother only
Biological Father Only	=1 if youth lives with biological father only
Stepparent	=1 if youth lives with one biological parent and one stepparent
Other Parent	=1 if youth lives with another parent figure (for example, a grandparent)
Residence	
Rural (ref. category)	=1 if youth lives in a rural area
Urban	=1 if youth lives in a urban area
Mother Supportive (1997 only)	=0 if youth views mother as not very supportive =1 if youth views mother as somewhat supportive

Table A-3. Variable definitions (continued)

Variable	Definition
Mother Permissive (1997 only)	=2 if youth views mother as very supportive =1 if youth views mother as permissive
Residences since Age 12	Number of differences residences since age 12
Schools since 7th Grade	Number of regular schools ever attended as of survey date
Region	
Northeast	=1 if youth lives in Northeast
North Central (ref. category)	=1 if youth lives in North Central (or Midwest)
South	=1 if youth lives in South
West	=1 if youth lives in West
Birth Cohort	
1980 (ref. category)	=1 if youth was born in 1980
1981	=1 if youth was born in 1981
1982	=1 if youth was born in 1982
1983	=1 if youth was born in 1983
1984	=1 if youth was born in 1984
School Performance	
GPA in 8th Grade, 8-Point Scale	=1 if mostly below Ds =2 if mostly Ds =3 if about half Cs and half Ds

Table A-3. Variable definitions (continued)

Variable	Definition
	=4 if mostly Cs
	=5 if about half Cs and half Bs
	=6 if mostly Bs
	=7 if about half Bs and half As
	=8 if mostly As
Ever Repeated a Grade	=1 if youth ever repeated a grade prior to the interview
School Attachment (1997 only)	Sum of four items asking youth how much they agree (1=strongly disagree to 4=strongly agree) about their school that: (1) teachers are good, (2) teachers are interested in students, (3) grading in fair, and (4) discipline is fair
Cognitive Ability ASVAB Math-Verbal Score	Youth's percentile score on four subtests of the Armed Services Vocational Aptitude Battery: Mathematical Knowledge, Arithmetic Reasoning, Word Knowledge, and Paragraph Comprehension
Peer Environment in 1997 Antisocial Peers	Average of five items asking youth what percentage of kids in their grade at school: (1) smoke cigarettes, (2) get drunk at least once a month, (3) belong to a gang, (4) use illegal drugs, and (5) cut classes or skip school

Table A-3. Variable definitions (continued)

Variable	Definition
Prosocial Peers	Average of four items asking youth what percentage of kids in their grade at school: (1) go to church, (2) participate in organized sports, clubs, or school activities, (3) plan to go to college, and (4) do volunteer work
Other Deviant Behavior	
Ever had Sex	=1 if youth has ever had sexual intercourse
Adult Role Transitions	
Ever had a Child	=1 if youth ever had a biological child
Worked > 20 Hours	=1 if youth worked more than 20 hours per week on average in the last calendar year
Ever Married	=1 if youth has ever been married
Living with a Sexual Partner	=1 if youth is living with an opposite-sex partner on the interview date
Survey Structure	
Months since Last Interview	Number of months that have elapsed since youth was last interviewed (or since birth at round 1)

Note: "**ref. category**" **indicates reference category in statistical models**

Table A-4. Items used to create delinquency and drug use scales

Item	Description
Delinquency	
Carrying a handgun	Carried a handgun (any firearm other than a rifle or shotgun)
Vandalism	Purposely damaged or destroyed property
Petty theft	Stole something worth less than $50
Petty shoplifting	Took something from a store worth less than $50
Petty larceny	Snatched someone's purse or wallet or picked someone's pocket to steal less than $50
Petty burglary	Went into a locked house or building to steal less than $50
Petty armed robbery	Used a weapon to steal less than $50
Major theft	Stole something worth more than $50
Major shoplifting	Took something from a store worth more than $50
Major larceny	Snatched someone's purse or wallet or picked someone's pocket to steal more than $50
Major burglary	Went into a locked house or building to steal less more $50
Major armed robbery	Used a weapon to steal more than $50
Vehicle theft	Stole a motor vehicle such as a car or motorcycle for own use or to sell it
Receiving income from stolen property	Amount of cash received from stolen items or would have received if sold them
Other property crimes	Fencing, receiving, possessing or selling stolen property, or cheating someone by selling them

Table A-4. Items used to create delinquency and drug use scales (continued)

Item	Description
	something that was worthless or worth much less than what it was
Income from other property crimes	Total cash income from other property crimes such as fencing, receiving, possessing or selling stolen property
Aggravated assault	Attacked someone with the idea of seriously hurting them or have a situation end up in a serious fight or assault of some kind
Selling illegal drugs	Sold or helped sell marijuana (pot, grass), hashish (hash) or other hard drugs such as heroin, cocaine or LSD
Selling marijuana	Sold marijuana or hashish, that is pot, grass or hash
Selling hard drugs	Sold or helped to sell hard drugs such as heroin, cocaine, LSD or other drugs
Income from selling drugs	Cash income made from selling or helping to sell marijuana, cocaine or other drugs
Drug Use	
Smoking cigarettes	Smoked a cigarette in the last 30 days
Smoking > 1 pack per day	Smoked more than 20 cigarettes per day in the last 30 days
Drinking alcohol	Drank alcohol in the last 30 days
Binge drinking	Had five or more drinks on the same occasion in the past 30 days
Drinking alcohol at school or work	Drank alcohol before or during school or work in the past 30

Table A-4. Items used to create delinquency and drug use scales (continued)

Item	Description
	days
Using marijuana	Used marijuana in the last 30 days
Using marijuana at school or work	Used marijuana before or during school or work in the past 30 days

Table A-5. Restrictions to obtain final NLSY97 sample

	N	Person-Years
Original Sample	8,984	62,888
Lagging independent variables	8,984	53,904
Valid Data on Dropout	8,812	48,144
Valid Data on Delinquency	8,697	45,614
Valid Data on Drug Use	8,694	45,367
Valid Data on 1996 Poverty Status	6,398	33,724
At Least Two Person-Years	6,211	33,537
% of Original Sample	69.1	53.3

Note: **Percentages are unweighted**

N = **number of individuals**

Table A- 6. Number of person-year observations contributed by youth

# of Person-Years	N	% of N	NT	% of NT
6	4,383	70.6	26,298	78.5
5	698	11.2	3,490	10.4
4	562	9.1	1,296	6.7
3	324	5.2	732	2.9
2	244	3.9	488	1.5

Note: **Percentages are unweighted**

N = number of individuals
NT = number of person-year observations

Table A- 7. Descriptive statistics, pooled

	All		Poor		Not Poor	
	Mean or %	S.D.	Mean or %	S.D.	Mean or %	S.D.
Dropout						
Dropout	13.2%		27.7%		10.4%	
Dropout (alternative definition)	9.7%		21.4%		7.4%	
Delinquency and Drug Use						
Delinquency	0.85	1.99	0.88	2.12	0.84	1.96
Drug Use	1.32	1.57	1.15	1.53	1.35	1.57
Social Sanctions						
Suspended from School	8.9%		14.5%		7.8%	
Arrested	5.8%		7.8%		5.4%	
Demographics						
Age	18.38	2.24	18.32	2.24	18.24	2.25
Gender						

Table A- 7. Descriptive statistics, pooled (continued)

	All		Poor		Not Poor	
	Mean or %	S.D.	Mean or %	S.D.	Mean or %	S.D.
Male	50.3%		49.8%		50.4%	
Female	49.7%		50.2%		49.6%	
Race						
White	69.7%		40.3%		75.5%	
Black	14.2%		31.4%		10.8%	
Hispanic	11.8%		24.8%		9.2%	
Asian	1.7%		0.9%		1.8%	
Other	2.7%		2.5%		2.7%	
Parental Education						
Dropout	11.8%		38.5%		6.8%	
High School	30.2%		36.5%		29.0%	
College	58.1%		24.9%		64.1%	
1996 Household Income (Log)						
Bottom Quartile	18.5%		92.4%		4.1%	
2nd Quartile	29.3%		7.6%		28.2%	
3rd Quartile	34.3%		0.0%		34.8%	
Top Quartile	36.4%		0.0%		37.0%	

Table A- 7. Descriptive statistics, pooled (continued)

	All		Poor		Not Poor	
	Mean or %	S.D.	Mean or %	S.D.	Mean or %	S.D.
Mother < 20 at Birth	11.6%		22.7%		9.4%	
Family Structure						
Both Biological Parents	47.1%		22.5%		51.9%	
Biological Mother Only	20.3%		41.1%		16.2%	
Biological Father Only	3.5%		3.8%		3.5%	
Stepparent	12.5%		9.9%		13.0%	
Other Parent	16.6%		22.7%		15.4%	
Residence						
Rural	29.5%		26.0%		30.3%	
Urban	70.7%		74.1%		70.0%	
Mother Supportive (1997 only)	2.76	.46	2.72	.49	2.77	.45

Table A- 7. Descriptive statistics, pooled (continued)

	All		Poor		Not Poor	
	Mean or %	S.D.	Mean or %	S.D.	Mean or %	S.D.
Mother Permissive (1997 only)	47.0%	.49	46.9%	.48	47.0%	.49
Residences since Age 12	2.56	2.18	3.21	2.68	2.44	2.05
Schools since 7th Grade	2.16	1.00	2.29	1.22	2.14	.94
Region						
Northeast	16.7%		17.0%		16.6%	
North Central	27.8%		19.7%		29.4%	
South	34.9%		42.6%		33.4%	
West	20.6%		20.7%		20.6%	
Birth Cohort						
1980	18.2%		16.6%		18.6%	
1981	19.1%		17.8%		19.3%	
1982	20.0%		21.1%		19.9%	
1983	20.6%		21.2%		20.5%	
1984	22.0%		23.3%		21.8%	

School Performance

Table A- 7. Descriptive statistics, pooled (continued)

	All		Poor		Not Poor	
	Mean or %	S.D.	Mean or %	S.D.	Mean or %	S.D.
GPA in 8th Grade, 8-Point Scale	5.76	1.73	5.15	1.69	5.88	1.71
Ever Repeated a Grade	19.2%		32.9%		16.5%	
School Attachment (1997)	8.04	2.02	7.71	2.11	8.11	2.00
Cognitive Ability ASVAB Math-Verbal Score						
Bottom Quintile	13.8%		35.8%		10.1%	
2nd Quintile	18.6%		36.6%		16.5%	
3rd Quintile	23.8%		27.7%		23.3%	
4th Quintile	27.1%		23.1%		27.6%	
Top Quintile	30.4%		12.6%		32.6%	
Peer Environment in 1997						
Antisocial Peers	2.14	.92	2.29	.98	2.11	.91

Table A- 7. Descriptive statistics, pooled (continued)

	All		Poor		Not Poor	
	Mean or %	S.D.	Mean or %	S.D.	Mean or %	S.D.
Prosocial Peers	3.06	.69	2.96	.75	3.08	.67
Other Deviant Behavior						
Ever had Sex	56.5%		64.4%		55.0%	
Adult Role Transitions						
Ever had a Child	6.9%		14.5%		5.5%	
Worked > 20 Hours	43.5%		42.1%		43.7%	
Ever Married	3.0%		4.3%		2.7%	
Living with a Sexual Partner	5.1%		6.8%		4.7%	
Survey Structure						
Months since Last Interview	40.93	61.00	41.15	60.74	40.93	61.00
N	6,211		1,438		4,773	
NT	33,473		7612		25,861	

S.D. = standard deviation; *N* = number of individuals; *NT* = number of person-year observations

Note: Data are weighted. Standard deviations are not adjusted for survey. Percentages for dummy variables may not add to 100 percent due to rounding and imputation.

Table A-8. Comparison of included and excluded youth in 1997

	Included		Excluded	
	Mean or %	S.D.	Mean or %	S.D.
Dropout				
Dropout	2.6%		2.3%	
Dropout (alternative definition)	2.5%		2.4%	
Delinquency and Drug Use				
Delinquency	2.39	6.52	2.04*	6.50
Drug Use	4.69	11.85	4.64	12.16
Social Sanctions				
Suspended from School	29.3%		29.4%	
Arrested	4.6%		4.2%	
Poverty Status	23.3%		23.2%	
Demographics				
Age	14.27	1.51	14.55***	1.51
Gender				
Male	51.2%		51.2%	
Female	51.2%		51.2%	
Race				
White	52.3%		42.0%***	
Black	24.7%		28.8%***	
Hispanic	19.7%		24.4%***	
Asian	1.2%		2.9%***	
Other	2.0%		2.0%***	
Parental Education				
High School Dropout	16.7%		22.4%***	

Table A-8. Comparison of included and excluded youth in 1997 (continued)

	Included		Excluded	
	Mean or %	S.D.	Mean or %	S.D.
High School	31.6%		30.8%	
College	51.7%		46.8%***	
1996 Household Income (Log)				
Bottom Quartile	25.4%		24.7%	
2nd Quartile	33.3%		28.8%	
3rd Quartile	33.8%		28.8%	
Top Quartile	33.0%		42.4%**	
Mother < 20 at Birth	13.7%		12.8%	
Family Structure				
Both Biological Parents	49.7%		47.7%	
Biological Mother Only	28.2%		28.3%	
Biological Father Only	3.2%		3.6%	
Stepparent	13.7%		13.0%	
Other Parent	5.2%		7.4%***	
Residence				
Rural	25.6%		19.2%***	
Urban	74.4%		80.8%***	
Mother Supportive	2.75	.49	2.75	.49
Mother Permissive	46.1%		43.6%*	
Residences since Age 12	1.55	1.01	1.53	1.07

Table A-8. Comparison of included and excluded youth in 1997 (continued)

	Included		Excluded	
	Mean or %	S.D.	Mean or %	S.D.
Schools since 7th Grade	1.45	.80	1.45	.81
Region				
Northeast	15.8%		21.9%***	
North Central	24.6%		18.8%***	
South	37.9%		36.1%	
West	21.7%		23.2%	
Birth Cohort				
1980	17.6%		21.6%***	
1981	20.5%		21.7%	
1982	20.2%		21.1%	
1983	21.1%		18.0%***	
1984	20.6%		17.7%***	
School Performance				
GPA in 8th Grade, 8-Point Scale	5.60	1.66	5.56	1.67
Ever Repeated a Grade	17.1%		16.0%	
School Attachment	7.94	1.98	7.88	1.98
Cognitive Ability ASVAB Math-Verbal Score				
Bottom Quintile	19.1%		22.3%**	
2nd Quintile	23.6%		29.0%***	
3rd Quintile	25.2%		24.6%	
4th Quintile	25.5%		23.7%	
Top Quintile	25.8%		22.7%*	

Table A-8. Comparison of included and excluded youth in 1997 (continued)

	Included		Excluded	
	Mean or %	S.D.	Mean or %	S.D.
Peer Environment				
Antisocial Peers	2.20	.94	2.26**	.94
Prosocial Peers	3.03	.73	3.01	.73
Other Deviant Behavior				
Ever had Sex	23.6%		26.0%*	
Adult Role Transitions				
Ever had a Child	1.0%		1.3%	
Work > 20 Hours	14.1%		15.3%	
Ever Married	0.0%		0.0%	
Living with a Sexual Partner	0.2%		0.1%	
N	6,211		2,773	

S.D. = standard deviation

N = number of individuals

Note: Data are unweighted. Percentages for dummy variables may not add to 100 percent due to rounding and missing data.

*** Excluded different from included at $p < .001$
** Excluded different from included at $p < .01$
* Excluded different from included at $p < .05$

Table A-9. Descriptive statistics for delinquency and drug use

		Survey Year						Within-Person
	Pooled	1997	1998	1999	2000	2001	2002	
Delinquency								
All								
Any in past year	28.8%	48.9%	32.8%	27.6%	24.2%	21.1%	18.3%	66.7%
Number of different	2.95	3.00	3.13	2.90	3.09	2.71	2.59	2.59
Poor								
Any in past year	29.8%	49.6%	34.7%	27.3%	26.1%	22.0%	18.5%	70.1%
Number of different	2.96	2.99	3.19	2.89	3.23	2.38	2.84	2.84
Not Poor								
Any in past year	28.7%	48.8%	32.4%	27.6%	23.8%	20.9%	18.2%	66.0%
Number of different	2.95	3.01	3.12	2.91	3.06	2.78	2.54	2.54
Drug Use								
All								

Table A-9. Descriptive statistics for delinquency and drug use (continued)

		Survey Year						Within-Person
	Pooled	1997	1998	1999	2000	2001	2002	
Any in past month	53.8%	27.2%	45.4%	54.3%	59.2%	66.4%	71.1%	84.0%
Number of different	2.45	2.24	2.39	2.47	2.49	2.51	2.46	2.25
Poor								
Any in past month	48.3%	27.3%	42.8%	50.2%	53.0%	57.7%	59.9%	80.5%
Number of different	2.38	2.14	2.29	2.40	2.47	2.45	2.37	2.11
Not Poor								
Any in past month	54.9%	27.2%	45.9%	55.1%	60.4%	68.2%	73.3%	84.7%
Number of different	2.46	2.26	2.40	2.48	2.49	2.52	2.47	2.27

Note: Data are weighted. Mean variety is calculated only for youth who reported engaging in any delinquency or drug use during the reference period. The pooled estimate is the mean across survey years. The within-person column gives person-specific estimates. For prevalence, this is the percentage of youth who ever engaged in delinquency or drug use. For variety, this is the mean variety of delinquency or drug use by youth in the years that they engaged in delinquency or drug use.

Table A-10. Comparison of dropouts and non-dropouts in 1997, by poverty status

	All		Poor		Not Poor	
	Dropouts	Non-Dropouts	Dropouts	Non-Dropouts	Dropouts	Non-Dropouts
Social Sanctions						
Suspended from School	57.2%***	20.1%	55.6%***	36.2%	58.0%***	17.3%
Arrested	11.7%***	2.8%	5.8%	4.4%	14.8%***	2.6%
Demographics						
Age	16.70***	15.82	16.72***	15.67	16.69***	15.84
Gender						
Male	52.8%	49.7%	54.2%	50.1%	56.5%	50.8%
Female	47.2%	50.3%	45.8%	49.9%	43.5%	49.2%
Race						
White	63.4%*	70.0%	47.0%*	39.3%	71.4%	75.5%
Black	18.5%**	13.9%	28.2%	31.6%	13.7%	10.7%
Hispanic	15.8%*	11.6%	23.6%	25.5%	12.0%	9.1%
Asian	0.0%*	1.8%	0.0%	1.0%	0.0%*	2.0%
Other Race	2.3%	2.7%	1.2%	2.7%	2.8%	2.7%

Parental Education

Table A-10. Comparison of dropouts and non-dropouts in 1997, by poverty status (continued)

	All		Poor		Not Poor	
	Dropouts	Non-Dropouts	Dropouts	Non-Dropouts	Dropouts	Non-Dropouts
College	37.1%***	59.0%	18.5%*	25.7%	46.2%***	64.6%
High School	35.8%**	30.1%	33.3%	36.9%	37.0%**	29.0%
High School Dropout	27.2%***	10.9%	48.2%**	37.4%	16.8%***	6.4%
Mother < 20 at Birth	18.1%***	11.4%	22.1%	23.4%	16.1%***	9.3%
Family Structure						
Both Biological Parents	31.8%***	55.5%	16.5%*	26.2%	39.3%***	60.8%
Biological Mother Only	34.1%***	23.5%	60.4%	54.7%	21.2%	17.9%
Biological Father Only	5.9%*	3.2%	4.9%	3.1%	6.4%**	3.2%
Stepparent	20.9%***	14.0%	12.6%	8.9%	24.9%***	15.0%
Other Parent	7.3%***	3.7%	5.7%	7.0%	8.1%***	3.2%
Residence						
Rural	30.1%	30.5%	25.0%	24.7%	32.7%	31.5%
Urban	71.7%	70.2%	75.2%	75.6%	69.9%	69.2%

Table A-10. Comparison of dropouts and non-dropouts in 1997, by poverty status (continued)

	All		Poor		Not Poor	
	Dropouts	Non-Dropouts	Dropouts	Non-Dropouts	Dropouts	Non-Dropouts
Mother Supportive	2.73	2.76	2.73	2.72	2.73	2.77
Mother Permissive	55.5%**	46.6%	54.1%*	45.2%	56.2%**	46.8%
Residences since Age 12	2.14***	1.48	2.49***	1.72	1.96***	1.43
Schools since 7th Grade	1.99***	1.43	199.1%***	129.0%	1.99***	1.45
Region						
Northeast	18.0%	17.0%	23.1%*	16.7%	15.3%	17.1%
North Central	25.8%	28.3%	26.3%*	19.7%	25.5%	29.9%
South	42.0%**	33.9%	37.3%	42.5%	44.4%***	32.3%
West	14.3%**	20.7%	13.3%*	21.0%	14.8%**	20.7%
Birth Cohort						
1980	34.7%	16.7%	34.0%***	12.9%	35.1%***	17.4%
1981	27.2%	18.5%	22.3%	17.1%	29.7%***	18.7%
1982	16.5%	20.4%	24.5%	21.3%	12.3%**	20.3%
1983	11.8%***	21.1%	11.1%***	22.9%	12.2%**	20.8%
1984	9.8%***	23.3%	8.2%***	25.8%	10.6%***	22.8%

School Performance

Table A-10. Comparison of dropouts and non-dropouts in 1997, by poverty status (continued)

	All		Poor		Not Poor	
	Dropouts	Non-Dropouts	Dropouts	Non-Dropouts	Dropouts	Non-Dropouts
GPA in 8th Grade, 8-Point Scale	3.18***	4.39	4.29***	3.80	4.54***	3.07
Ever Repeated a Grade	42.5%***	12.4%	42.5%***	22.3%	42.5%***	10.6%
School Attachment	7.11***	8.09	7.00***	7.82	7.16***	8.14
Cognitive Ability ASVAB Math-Verbal Score						
Bottom Quintile	34.5%***	12.6%	50.8%***	33.1%	27.4%***	9.4%
2nd Quintile	36.1%***	18.0%	38.0%	36.7%	35.6%***	15.8%
3rd Quintile	31.4%	23.7%	26.8%	28.2%	32.7%**	23.2%
4th Quintile	23.1%***	27.6%	28.7%	22.5%	21.4%	28.2%
Top Quintile	9.4%***	30.7%	6.5%	12.7%	10.3%***	32.7%
Peer Environment						
Antisocial Peers	2.78***	2.10	2.87***	2.21	2.74***	2.09
Prosocial Peers	2.74***	3.08	2.66***	3.00	2.78***	3.10

Other Deviant Behavior

Table A-10. Comparison of dropouts and non-dropouts in 1997, by poverty status (continued)

	All		Poor		Not Poor	
	Dropouts	Non-Dropouts	Dropouts	Non-Dropouts	Dropouts	Non-Dropouts
Ever had Sex	56.1%***	18.2%	59.9%***	24.9%	54.2%***	17.0%
Adult Role Transitions						
Ever had a Child	4.3%***	0.4%	6.7%***	1.1%	3.1%***	0.3%
Worked > 20 Hours	33.8%***	13.4%	27.6%***	10.7%	36.9%***	13.9%
Ever Married	0.4%	0.0%	1.1%**	0.1%	0.0%***	0.0%
Living with a Sexual Partner	1.5%***	0.0%	1.7%***	0.1%	1.4%***	0.0%
Survey Structure						
Months since Birth	185.90***	175.93	185.56***	173.79	186.08***	176.31
N	396	5,167	167	1,117	229	4,050

Note: Data are weighted. Percentages for dummy variables may not add to 100 percent due to rounding and imputation.

*** Dropouts different from non-dropouts at $p < .001$ ** $p < .01$ * $p < .05$

Table A-11. Dropout status in 1998 by delinquency in 1997, by poverty status

	All		Poor		Not Poor	
	Dropouts	Non-Dropouts	Dropouts	Non-Dropouts	Dropouts	Non-Dropouts
Any Delinquency						
Any in past year	65.2%***	47.8%	58.6%***	48.2%	68.6%***	47.7%***
Number of different	4.07***	2.90	3.92***	2.82	4.14***	2.92***
Individual Offenses						
Carrying a handgun	17.5%***	8.2%	22.3%***	8.7%	15.1%***	8.2%
Vandalism	34.0%*	26.2%	30.1%	25.3%	36.0%**	26.4%
Petty theft	40.8%***	30.6%	33.3%	28.7%	44.7%***	31.0%
Petty shoplifting	36.1%***	25.2%	30.7%*	23.0%	38.9%***	25.6%
Petty larceny	2.5%*	1.1%	1.5%	1.3%	3.0%***	1.0%
Petty burglary	5.6%***	1.6%	4.9%***	1.8%	6.0%***	1.6%

Table A-11. Dropout status in 1998 by delinquency in 1997, by poverty status (continued)

	All		Poor		Not Poor	
	Dropouts	Non-Dropouts	Dropouts	Non-Dropouts	Dropouts	Non-Dropouts
Petty armed robbery	1.0%*	0.3%	1.2%***	0.8%	0.9%***	0.3%
Major Theft	9.8%***	4.0%	7.7%***	3.6%	10.9%***	4.1%
Major shoplifting	7.5%***	2.7%	7.0%***	2.5%	7.7%***	2.7%
Major larceny	0.7%	0.4%	1.8%***	0.5%	0.2%***	0.4%
Major burglary	2.9%**	1.0%	3.7%***	0.8%	2.5%***	1.0%
Major armed robbery	.	.	.	.	.	.
Vehicle theft	3.6%***	0.7%	3.2%***	0.6%	3.8%***	0.7%
Income from stolen property	8.7%***	2.9%	6.4%***	2.7%	9.9%***	2.9%
Other property crimes	9.1%***	4.0%	8.4%***	4.0%	9.5%***	4.0%
Income from other property crimes	6.0%***	2.8%	4.9%***	2.6%	6.6%***	2.8%
Aggravated	34.5%***	14.4%	30.9%**	19.8%	36.3%***	13.4%

Table A-11. Dropout status in 1998 by delinquency in 1997, by poverty status (continued)

	All		Poor		Not Poor	
	Dropouts	Non-Dropouts	Dropouts	Non-Dropouts	Dropouts	Non-Dropouts
assault						
Selling illegal drugs	14.3%***	4.2%	9.1%***	3.1%	17.0%***	4.4%
Selling marijuana	12.3%***	3.3%	8.7%***	2.1%	14.2%***	3.5%
Selling hard drugs	7.2%***	1.7%	4.9%***	1.6%	8.4%***	1.8%
income from selling drugs	10.9%***	2.9%	7.6%***	1.9%	12.7%***	3.1%

Note: Data are weighted. The reference period for 1997 is birth to the round 1 interview. Mean variety is calculated only for youth who reported engaging in any delinquency during the reference period.

*** Dropouts different from non-dropouts at $p < .001$
** Dropouts different from non-dropouts at $p < .01$
* Dropouts different from non-dropouts at $p < .05$

Table A-12. Dropout status in 1998 by drug use in 1997, by poverty status

	All Youth		Poor		Not Poor	
	Dropouts	Non-Dropouts	Dropouts	Non-Dropouts	Dropouts	Non-Dropouts
Any Drug Use						
Any in past month	52.6%	25.4%	51.9%	23.5%	52.9%	25.8%
Number of Different	2.49	2.21	2.49	2.03	2.49	2.24
Individual Drug Use						
Smoking cigarettes	44.0%***	15.5%	46.4%***	14.0%	42.8%***	15.7%
Smoking >1 pack per day	1.5%***	0.2%	2.7%***	0.2%	0.9%***	0.2%
Drinking alcohol	29.6%***	18.0%	29.9%***	14.0%	29.5%**	18.7%
Binge drinking	8.9%***	3.9%	5.5%***	3.9%	10.6%***	3.9%
Drinking alcohol at school or work	17.5%***	8.3%	17.3%***	6.4%	17.6%***	8.6%
Using marijuana	19.9%***	7.5%	18.6%***	6.6%	20.6%***	7.6%
Using marijuana at school or work	9.5%***	2.8%	8.5%***	2.4%	10.0%***	2.9%

Note: Data are weighted. The reference period for 1997 is the past month. Mean variety is calculated only for youth who reported engaging in any drug use during the reference period.

*** Dropouts different from non-dropouts at $p < .001$
** Dropouts different from non-dropouts at $p < .01$
* Dropouts different from non-dropouts at $p < .05$

Table A-13. Regressions of dropout on delinquency

	Model 1 Panel Logit No Controls	Model 2 Panel Logit Controls	Model 3 Hybrid Random Effects	
			Between	Within
Delinquency	.141***	.057***	.123***	.007
	(.009)	(.011)	(.019)	(.009)
Demographics				
Male		.335***	.397***	
		(.071)	(.064)	
Race				
Black		-.440***	-.401***	
		(.093)	(.081)	
Hispanic		-.112	-.105	
		(.104)	(.087)	
Asian		-.013	.188	
		(.598)	(.405)	
Other		-.114	-.126	
		(.277)	(.216)	
Parental Education		-.098***	-.105***	
		(.014)	(.012)	
1996 Household Income (Log)		-.118***	-.115***	
		(.019)	(.016)	

Table A-13. Regressions of dropout on delinquency (continued)

	Model 1 Panel Logit No Controls	Model 2 Panel Logit Controls	Model 3 Hybrid Random Effects	
			Between	Within
Mother < 20 at Birth		.056	.061	
		(.090)	(.075)	
Family Structure				
Biological Mother Only		.305***	.367***	-.030
		(.085)	(.092)	(.095)
Biological Father Only		.712***	.980***	.087
		(.161)	(.185)	(.141)
Stepparent		.248*	.216	-.008
		(.104)	(.113)	(.113)
Other Parent		.420***	.687***	-.099
		(.091)	(.122)	(.091)
Urban		.035	.119	-.025
		(.078)	(.084)	(.080)
Mother Supportive (1997 only)		.061	.114	
		(.070)	(.059)	
Mother Permissive (1997 only)		.105	.109	
		(.070)	(.058)	
Residences since Age 12		.131***	.140***	-.005
		(.016)	(.015)	(.019)

Table A-13. Regressions of dropout on delinquency (continued)

	Model 1 Panel Logit No Controls	Model 2 Panel Logit Controls	Model 3 Hybrid Random Effects	
			Between	Within
Schools since 7th Grade		.129***	.012	.562***
		(.033)	(.031)	(.049)
School Performance				
GPA in 8th Grade, 8-Point Scale		-.298***	-.316***	
		(.023)	(.019)	
Ever Repeated a Grade		.962***	.938***	.785***
		(.076)	(.069)	(.120)
School Attachment (1997 only)		-.038*	-.032*	
		(.018)	(.014)	
Cognitive Ability				
ASVAB Math-Verbal Score		-.014***	-.015***	
		(.002)	(.001)	
Peer Environment in 1997				
Antisocial Peers		.199***	.143***	
		(.043)	(.034)	
Prosocial Peers		-.097	-.082*	
		(.052)	(.041)	
Other Deviant Behavior				

Table A-13. Regressions of dropout on delinquency (continued)

	Model 1 Panel Logit No Controls	Model 2 Panel Logit Controls	Model 3 Hybrid Random Effects	
			Between	Within
Ever had Sex		.843***	1.227***	.198**
		(.082)	(.120)	(.075)
Adult Roles Transitions				
Ever had a Child		1.047***	1.477***	.129
		(.087)	(.119)	(.076)
Worked > 20 Hours		.216***	.285*	.109*
		(.054)	(.115)	(.046)
Ever Married		.150	.564***	-.161
		(.143)	(.210)	(.122)
Living with a Sexual Partner		.368***	1.171***	.069
		(.094)	(.195)	(.080)

Note: Estimates are unweighted. Standard errors are in parentheses. Standard errors are corrected for clustering. All models include dummy variable controls for survey year, age, region of residence, and birth cohort. Coefficients are omitted to simplify presentation.

*** $p < .001$ ** $p < .01$ * $p < .05$

Table A-14. Regressions of dropout on drug use

	Model 1 Panel Logit No Controls	Model 2 Panel Logit Controls	Model 3 Hybrid Random Effects	
			Between	Within
Drug Use	.219***	.181***	.317***	.056***
	(.018)	(.020)	(.033)	(.018)
Demographics				
Male		.336***	.433***	
		(.071)	(.062)	
Race				
Black		-.334***	-.235**	
		(.095)	(.083)	
Hispanic		-.059	-.016	
		(.104)	(.087)	
Asian		.028	.252	
		(.594)	(.401)	
Other		-.081	-.074	
		(.274)	(.214)	
Parental Education		-.102	-.110***	
		(.014)	(.012)	
1996 Household Income (Log)		-.122***	-.116***	
		(.019)	(.016)	

Table A-14. Regressions of dropout on drug use (continued)

	Model 1 Panel Logit No Controls	Model 2 Panel Logit Controls	Model 3 Hybrid Random Effects	
			Between	Within
Mother < 20 at Birth		.074***	.081	
		(.090)	(.075)	
Family Structure				
Biological Mother Only		.312***	.392***	-.028
		(.085)	(.092)	(.095)
Biological Father Only		.700***	.954***	.080
		(.161)	(.185)	(.142)
Stepparent		.267**	.259*	-.007
		(.104)	(.112)	(.114)
Other Parent		.433***	.752***	-.098
		(.091)	(.122)	(.092)
Urban		.024	.101	-.033
		(.078)	(.083)	(.081)
Mother Supportive (1997 only)		.054	.099	
		(.070)	(.058)	
Mother Permissive (1997 only)		.101	.104	
		(.070)	(.058)	
Residences since Age 12		.129***	.139***	-.006
		(.016)	(.015)	(.019)

Table A-14. Regressions of dropout on drug use (continued)

	Model 1 Panel Logit No Controls	Model 2 Panel Logit Controls	Model 3 Hybrid Random Effects	
			Between	Within
Schools since 7th Grade		.131***	.017***	.570***
		(.034)	(.031)	(.050)
School Performance				
GPA in 8th Grade, 8-Point Scale		-.294***	-.312***	
		(.023)	(.019)	
Ever Repeated a Grade		.967***	.946***	.784***
		(.076)	(.069)	(.121)
School Attachment (1997 only)		-.039*	-.034*	
		(.019)	(.014)	
Cognitive Ability				
ASVAB Math-Verbal Score		-.015***	-.015***	
		(.002)	(.001)	
Peer Environment in 1997				
Antisocial Peers		.192***	.140***	
		(.043)	(.034)	
Prosocial Peers		-.097	-.083*	
		(.052)	(.041)	
Other Deviant Behavior				

Table A-14. Regressions of dropout on drug use (continued)

	Model 1 Panel Logit No Controls	Model 2 Panel Logit Controls	Model 3 Hybrid Random Effects	
			Between	Within
Ever had Sex		.763***	1.039***	.183*
		(.082)	(.122)	(.076)
Adult Roles Transition				
Ever had a Child		1.086***	1.588***	.139
		(.088)	(.120)	(.077)
Worked > 20 Hours		.184***	.192***	.103*
		(.054)	(.114)	(.047)
Ever Married		.207	.663**	-.152
		(.144)	(.210)	(.123)
Living with a Sexual Partner		.381***	1.159***	.079
		(.094)	(.195)	(.080)

Note: Estimates are unweighted. Standard errors are in parentheses. Standard errors are corrected for clustering. All models include dummy variable controls for survey year, age, region of residence, and birth cohort. Coefficients are omitted to simplify presentation.

*** $p < .001$ ** $p < .01$ * $p < .05$

Table A-15. Regressions of dropout on delinquency and drug use

	Model 1 Panel Logit No Controls	Model 2 Panel Logit Controls	Model 3 Hybrid Random Effects	
			Between	Within
Delinquency	.109***	.033**	.061**	.003
	(.009)	(.011)	(.020)	(.009)
Drug Use	.159***	.165***	.277***	.056**
	(.018)	(.021)	(.035)	(.019)
Demographics				
Male		.326***	.376***	
		(.071)	(.064)	
Race				
Black		-.349***	-.267**	
		(.094)	(.082)	
Hispanic		-.066	-.028	
		(.104)	(.087)	
Asian		.031	.203	
		(.591)	(.404)	
Other		-.076	-.110	
		(.273)	(.216)	
Parental Education		-.102***	-.111***	
		(.014)	(.012)	

Table A-15. Regressions of dropout on delinquency and drug use (continued)

	Model 1 Panel Logit No Controls	Model 2 Panel Logit Controls	Model 3 Hybrid Random Effects	
			Between	Within
1996 Household Income		-.121	-.117***	
(Log)		(.019)	(.016)	
Mother < 20 at Birth		.073	.106	
		(.090)	(.074)	
Family Structure				
Biological Mother		.317***	.389***	-.025
Only		(.085)	(.092)	(.095)
Biological Father		.709***	.979***	.090
Only		(.161)	(.185)	(.141)
Stepparent		.265*	.253**	.001
		(.104)	(.113)	(.114)
Other Parent		.435***	.714***	-.083
		(.091)	(.122)	(.092)
Urban		.024	.109	-.033
		(.078)	(.084)	(.081)
Mother Supportive		.052	.113	
(1997 only)		(.070)	(.059)	
Mother Permissive		.101	.096	
(1997 only)		(.070)	(.058)	

Table A-15. Regressions of dropout on delinquency and drug use (continued)

	Model 1 Panel Logit No Controls	Model 2 Panel Logit Controls	Model 3 Hybrid Random Effects	
			Between	Within
Residences since Age 12		.127***	.130***	.005
		(.016)	(.015)	(.019)
Schools since 7th Grade		.131***	.006	.582***
		(.034)	(.031)	(.048)
School Performance				
GPA in 8th Grade, 8-Point Scale		-.295***	-.311	
		(.023)	(.019)	
Ever Repeated a Grade		.967***	.919***	.802***
		(.076)	(.069)	(.120)
School Attachment (1997 only)		-.037*	-.032	
		(.019)	(.014)	
Cognitive Ability				
ASVAB Math-Verbal Score		-.014***	-.015	
		(.002)	(.001)	
Peer Environment in 1997				
Antisocial Peers		.190***	.130	
		(.043)	(.035)	

Table A-15. Regressions of dropout on delinquency and drug use (continued)

	Model 1 Panel Logit No Controls	Model 2 Panel Logit Controls	Model 3 Hybrid Random Effects	
			Between	Within
Prosocial Peers		-.098***	-.084	
		(.052)	(.041)	
Other Deviant Behavior				
Ever had Sex		.768***	.977***	.230
		(.083)	(.120)	(.075)
Adult Roles Transition				
Ever had a Child		1.088***	1.553***	.160*
		(.088)	(.119)	(.077)
Worked > 20 Hours		.187***	.178	.117*
		(.054)	(.113)	(.046)
Ever Married		.209	.655**	-.138
		(.144)	(.211)	(.123)
Living with a Sexual		.390***	1.171***	.081**
Partner		(.094)	(.194)	(.080)

Note: Estimates are unweighted. Standard errors are in parentheses. Standard errors are corrected for clustering. All models include dummy variable controls for survey year, age, region of residence, and birth cohort. Coefficients are omitted to simplify presentation.

*** *p* < .001 ** *p* < .01 * *p* < .05

Table A-16. Summary of regressions of dropout on delinquency, by offense type

	Prevalence				Frequency			
	Model 1 Panel Logit No Controls	Model 2 Panel Logit Controls	Model 3 Hybrid Random Effects		Model 1 Panel Logit No Controls	Model 2 Panel Logit Controls	Model 3 Hybrid Random Effects	
			Between	Within			Between	Within
Carrying a handgun	+	+	+	NS	+	+	NS	NS
Vandalism	+	+	+	NS	+	NS	+	NS
Petty theft	+	+	+	NS	+	NS	NS	NS
Petty shoplifting	+	NS	+	NS				
Petty larceny	+	NS	+	NS				
Petty burglary	+	+	+	NS				
Petty armed robbery	+	+	+	NS				
Major theft	+	+	+	NS	+	+	+	NS
Major shoplifting	+	+	+	NS				
Major larceny	+	NS	+	NS				

Table A-16. Summary of regressions of dropout on delinquency, by offense type (continued)

	Prevalence				Frequency			
	Model 1 Panel Logit No Controls	Model 2 Panel Logit Controls	Model 3 Hybrid Random Effects		Model 1 Panel Logit No Controls	Model 2 Panel Logit Controls	Model 3 Hybrid Random Effects	
			Between	Within			Between	Within
Major burglary	+	+	+	NS				
Major armed robbery	+	+	+	NS				
Vehicle theft	+	+	+	NS				
Receiving income from stolen property	+	+	+	NS				
Other property crimes	+	+	+	NS	+	+	+	NS
Income from other property crimes	+	+	+	NS				
Aggravated assault	+	+	+	NS	+	+	+	NS
Selling illegal drugs	+	+	+	NS	+	+	+	NS
Selling marijuana	+	+	+	NS				

Table A-16. Summary of regressions of dropout on delinquency, by offense type (continued)

	Prevalence				Frequency			
	Model 1 Panel Logit No Controls	Model 2 Panel Logit Controls	Model 3 Hybrid Random Effects		Model 1 Panel Logit No Controls	Model 2 Panel Logit Controls	Model 3 Hybrid Random Effects	
			Between	**Within**			**Between**	**Within**
Selling hard drugs	+	+	+	NS				
Income from selling drugs	+	+	+	NS				

Note: Model 1 includes no control variables (except dummy variables for survey year, age, region, and birth year, and a continuous variable for exposure time). Model 2 includes all controls. "+" indicates that the coefficient is positive and statistically significant ($p < .05$). "-" indicates that the coefficient is negative and statistically significant ($p < .05$). NS indicates that the coefficient is not statistically significant.

Table A-17. Summary of regressions of dropout on drug use, by drug type

	Prevalence				Frequency			
	Model 1 Panel Logit No Controls	Model 2 Panel Logit Controls	Model 3 Hybrid Random Effects		Model 1 Panel Logit No Controls	Model 2 Panel Logit Controls	Model 3 Hybrid Random Effects	
			Between	Within			Between	Within
Cigarette smoking	+	+	+	+	+	+	+	+
Smoking > 1 pack/day	+	+	+	NS				
Alcohol	NS	NS	NS	NS	+	NS	NS	NS
Binge drinking	+	+	+	NS	+	+	+	+
Drinking alcohol at school or work	+	+	+	NS	+	+	+	NS
Using marijuana	+	+	+	+	+	+	+	+
Using marijuana at school or work	+	+	+	NS	+	+	+	NS

Note: Model 1 includes no control variables (except dummy variables for survey year, age, region, and birth year, and a continuous variable for exposure time). Model 2 includes all controls. "+" indicates that the coefficient is positive and statistically significant ($p < .05$). "-" indicates that the coefficient is negative and statistically significant ($p < .05$). NS indicates that the coefficient is not statistically significant.

Table A-18. Summary of alternative model specifications for delinquency

| | Variety | | | | Frequency | | | |
| | Model 1 Panel Logit No Controls | Model 2 Panel Logit Controls | Model 3 Hybrid Random Effects | | Model 1 Panel Logit No Controls | Model 2 Panel Logit Controls | Model 3 Hybrid Random Effects | |
			Between	Within			Between	Within
Quadratic								
Delinquency	+	+	+	NS	+	+	NS	NS
Delinquency squared	-	NS	-	NS	NS	-	NS	NS
Binary								
Any v. none	+	+	+	NS				
Ordinal								
Variety 1-3 offenses	+	+	+	NS				

Table A-18. Summary of alternative model specifications for delinquency (continued)

	Variety				Frequency			
	Model 1 Panel Logit No Controls	Model 2 Panel Logit Controls	Model 3 Hybrid Random Effects		Model 1 Panel Logit No Controls	Model 2 Panel Logit Controls	Model 3 Hybrid Random Effects	
			Between	Within			Between	Within
4-6 offenses	+	+	+	NS				
6-9 offenses	+	+	+	NS				
10-12 offenses	+	+	+	NS				
>12 offenses	+	+	+	NS				
Ordinal								
Frequency								
1-5 times					+	+	+	NS
6-10 times					+	+	+	NS

Table A-18. Summary of alternative model specifications for delinquency (continued)

	Variety				Frequency			
	Model 1 Panel Logit No Controls	Model 2 Panel Logit Controls	Model 3 Hybrid Random Effects		Model 1 Panel Logit No Controls	Model 2 Panel Logit Controls	Model 3 Hybrid Random Effects	
			Between	Within			Between	Within
10-15 times					+	+	+	NS
>10 times					+	+	+	NS
Lag								
Past year	+	+	+	NS	+	+	+	NS
2 years ago	+	+	+	NS	+	+	+	NS
3 years ago	+	+	+	NS	+	+	+	+
Cap								
Variety								
15	+	+	+	NS				
10	+	+	+	NS				

Table A-18. Summary of alternative model specifications for delinquency (continued)

	Variety				Frequency			
	Model 1 Panel Logit No Controls	Model 2 Panel Logit Controls	Model 3 Hybrid Random Effects Between	Within	Model 1 Panel Logit No Controls	Model 2 Panel Logit Controls	Model 3 Hybrid Random Effects Between	Within
5	+	+	+	NS				
Cap								
Frequency								
50					+	+	+	NS
40					+	+	+	NS
30					+	+	+	NS
20					+	+	+	NS
10					+	+	+	NS
Log delinquency	+	+	+	NS	+	+	+	NS

Note: Model 1 includes no control variables (except dummy variables for survey year, age, region, and birth year, and a continuous variable for exposure time). Model 2 includes all controls. "+" indicates that the coefficient is positive and statistically significant ($p < .05$). "-" indicates that the coefficient is negative and statistically significant ($p < .05$). NS indicates that the coefficient is not statistically significant.

Table A-19. Summary of alternative model specifications for drug use

| | Variety | | | | Frequency | | | |
	Model 1 Panel Logit No Controls	Model 2 Panel Logit Controls	Model 3 Hybrid Random Effects		Model 1 Panel Logit No Controls	Model 2 Panel Logit Controls	Model 3 Hybrid Random Effects	
			Between	Within			Between	Within
Quadratic								
Drug use	+	+	+	+	+	+	+	+
Drug use squared	-	-	+	NS	-	-	+	NS
Binary								
Any use v. no use	+	+	+	+				
Ordinal								
Variety								

Table A-19. Summary of alternative model specifications for drug use (continued)

	Variety				Frequency			
	Model 1 Panel Logit No Controls	Model 2 Panel Logit Controls	Model 3 Hybrid Random Effects		Model 1 Panel Logit No Controls	Model 2 Panel Logit Controls	Model 3 Hybrid Random Effects	
			Between	**Within**			**Between**	**Within**
1	+	+	+	NS				
2	+	+	NS	NS				
3	+	+	+	+				
4	+	+	+	+				
5	+	+	+	+				
6	+	+	+	NS				
7	+	+	+	NS				
Ordinal Frequency Less than 15					NS	NS	NS	NS

Table A-19. Summary of alternative model specifications for drug use (continued)

	Variety				Frequency			
	Model 1 Panel Logit No Controls	Model 2 Panel Logit Controls	Model 3 Hybrid Random Effects Between	Within	Model 1 Panel Logit No Controls	Model 2 Panel Logit Controls	Model 3 Hybrid Random Effects Between	Within
16 to 30					+	+	+	+
More than 30					+	+	+	+
Lag								
Past month	+	+	+	+	+	+	+	+
2 years ago	+	+	NS	NS	+	+	NS	NS
3 years ago	+	+	NS	NS	+	+	NS	NS
Top-coded Frequency								
90					+	+	+	+
60					+	+	+	+

Table A-19. Summary of alternative model specifications for drug use (continued)

	Variety				Frequency			
	Model 1 Panel Logit No Controls	Model 2 Panel Logit Controls	Model 3 Hybrid Random Effects Between	Within	Model 1 Panel Logit No Controls	Model 2 Panel Logit Controls	Model 3 Hybrid Random Effects Between	Within
30					+	+	+	NS

Note: Model 1 includes no control variables (except dummy variables for survey year, age, region, and birth year, and a continuous variable for exposure time). Model 2 includes all controls. "+" indicates that the coefficient is positive and statistically significant ($p < .05$). "-" indicates that the coefficient is negative and statistically significant ($p < .05$). NS indicates that the coefficient is not statistically significant.

Table A-20. Regressions of dropout on delinquency, interaction with poverty status

	Model 1 Panel Logit No Controls	Model 2 Panel Logit Controls	Model 3 Hybrid Random Effects	
			Between	Within
Delinquency	.159***	.060***	.123***	.007
	(.011)	(.013)	(.015)	(.013)
Poverty Status	1.268***	.638***	.320***	
	(.069)	(.084)	(.060)	
Interaction				
Delinquency * Poverty	-.043*	-.016	.006	-.005
Status	(.019)	(.021)	(.026)	(.022)

Note: Estimates are unweighted. Standard errors are in parentheses and corrected for clustering. Model 1 includes no control variables (except dummy variables for survey year, age, region, and birth year, and a continuous variable for exposure time). Model 2 includes all controls.

*** $p < .001$ ** $p < .01$ * $p < .05$

Table A-21. Regressions of dropout on drug use, interaction with poverty status

	Model 1 Panel Logit No Controls	Model 2 Panel Logit Controls	Model 3 Hybrid Random Effects	
			Between	Within
Drug Use	.238***	.144***	.225***	.055**
	(.018)	(.020)	(.022)	(.021)
Poverty Status	1.291***	.332**	.239***	
	(.079)	(.109)	(.072)	
Interaction				
Drug Use * Poverty	.004	.021	.070*	-.015
Status	(.031)	(.035)	(.034)	(.035)

Note: Estimates are unweighted. Standard errors are in parentheses and corrected for clustering. Model 1 includes no control variables (except dummy variables for survey year, age, region, and birth year, and a continuous variable for exposure time). Model 2 includes all controls.

*** $p < .001$ ** $p < .01$ * $p < .05$

Table A-22. Summary of regressions of dropout on delinquency and drug use, interaction with alternative measure of poverty status

	Delinquency				Drug Use			
	Model 1 Panel Logit No Controls	Model 2 Panel Logit Controls	Model 3 Hybrid Random Effects		Model 1 Panel Logit No Controls	Model 2 Panel Logit Controls	Model 3 Hybrid Random Effects	
			Between	Within			Between	Within
Delinquency/Drug Use	+	+	+	+	+	+	+	+
2 X Poverty Level	-	-	-		-	-	-	
3 X Poverty Level	-	-	-		-	-	-	
4 X Poverty Level or More	-	-	-		-	-	-	
Delinquency/Drug Use * 2 X Poverty Level	+	NS	+	NS	+	NS	+	NS
Delinquency/Drug Use * 3 X Poverty Level	+	NS	+	NS	+	NS	+	NS
Delinquency/Drug Use * 4 X Poverty Level or More	+	NS	+	NS	+	NS	+	NS

Note: Model 1 includes no control variables. Model 2 includes all controls. "+" indicates that the coefficient is positive and statistically significant ($p < .05$). "-" indicates that the coefficient is negative and statistically significant ($p < .05$). NS indicates that the coefficient is not statistically significant.

Table A-23. Regressions of dropout on delinquency, interactions with social sanctions

	Model 1 Panel Logit No Controls	Model 2 Panel Logit Controls	Model 3 Hybrid Random Effects	
			Between	Within
Delinquency	.115***	.058***	.166***	-.001
	(.013)	(.014)	(.024)	(.012)
Social Sanctions				
Suspended from School	.928***	.218**	1.098***	-.130
	(.069)	(.079)	(.146)	(.073)
Arrested	1.186***	.706***	2.301***	.107
	(.071)	(.083)	(.174)	(.077)
Interactions				
Delinquency * Suspended from School	-.063***	-.040*	-.276***	.019
	(.016)	(.018)	(.062)	(.026)
Delinquency * Arrested	-.054**	-.037	-.269***	.028
	(.016)	(.019)	(.052)	(.027)

Note: Estimates are unweighted. Standard errors are in parentheses. Standard errors are corrected for clustering. Model 1 includes no control variables (except dummy variables for survey year, age, region, and birth year, and a continuous variable for exposure time). Model 2 includes all controls. Coefficients are omitted to simplify presentation.

*** $p < .001$ ** $p < .01$ * $p < .05$

Table A-24. Regressions of dropout on drug use, interactions with social sanctions

	Model 1 Panel Logit No Controls	Model 2 Panel Logit Controls	Model 3 Hybrid Random Effects	
			Between	Within
Drug Use	.182***	.151***	.249***	.049**
	(.016)	(.018)	(.026)	(.017)
Social Sanctions				
Suspended from	.856***	.144	.707***	-.140
School	(.077)	(.089)	(.179)	(.073)
Arrested	1.557***	.848***	2.753***	.111
	(.093)	(.109)	(.225)	(.076)
Interactions				
Drug Use *	-.035	-.016	-.012	-.030
Suspended from	(.028)	(.031)	(.087)	(.050)
School				
Drug Use * Arrested	-.194***	-.109**	-.542***	-.034
	(.031)	(.036)	(.086)	(.057)

Note: Estimates are unweighted. Standard errors are in parentheses. Standard errors are corrected for clustering. Model 1 includes no control variables (except dummy variables for survey year, age, region, and birth year, and a continuous variable for exposure time). Model 2 includes all controls. Coefficients are omitted to simplify presentation.

*** $p < .001$ ** $p < .01$ * $p < .05$

Table A-25. Regressions of dropout on delinquency, interactions with social sanctions and poverty status

	Model 1 Panel Logit No Controls	Model 2 Panel Logit Controls	Model 3 Hybrid Random Effects	
			Between	Within
Delinquency	.127***	.051**	.159***	-.005
	(.016)	(.017)	(.029)	(.014)
Social Sanctions				
Suspended from School	1.131***	.358***	1.489***	-.045
	(.087)	(.097)	(.186)	(.089)
Arrested	1.200***	.683***	2.389***	.097
	(.090)	(.105)	(.215)	(.095)
Social Class				
Poverty Status	1.313***	.405***	.484***	
	(.073)	(.105)	(.077)	
Interactions				
Delinquency * Suspended from School	-.071***	-.043	-.288***	.024
	(.020)	(.023)	(.077)	(.032)
Delinquency * Arrested	-.048*	-.017	-.291***	.074*
	(.020)	(.024)	(.061)	(.033)
Delinquency * Poverty Status	-.006	.021	.020	.014
	(.027)	(.030)	(.048)	(.024)

Table A-25. Regressions of dropout on delinquency, interactions with social sanctions and poverty status (continued)

	Model 1 Panel Logit No Controls	Model 2 Panel Logit Controls	Model 3 Hybrid Random Effects	
			Between	Within
Suspended from School * Poverty Status	-.769***	-.358*	-.956***	-.210
	(.127)	(.143)	(.282)	(.136)
Arrested * Poverty Status	-.100	.075	-.204	.023
	(.152)	(.174)	(.353)	(.162)
Delinquency * Suspended from School * Poverty Status	.018	-.001	-.005	-.022
	(.034)	(.038)	(.133)	(.053)
Delinquency * Arrested * Poverty Status	-.032	-.060	.105	-.143*
	(.035)	(.039)	(.119)	(.058)

Note: Estimates are unweighted. Standard errors are in parentheses. Standard errors are corrected for clustering. Model 1 includes no control variables (except dummy variables for survey year, age, region, and birth year, and a continuous variable for exposure time). Model 2 includes all controls. Coefficients are omitted to simplify presentation.

*** $p < .001$ ** $p < .01$ * $p < .05$

Table A-26. Regressions of dropout on drug use, interactions with social sanctions and poverty status

	Model 1 Panel Logit No Controls	Model 2 Panel Logit Controls	Model 3 Hybrid Random Effects Between	Model 3 Hybrid Random Effects Within
Drug Use	.069***	.018	.212***	.056**
	(.011)	(.011)	(.031)	(.022)
Social Sanctions				
Suspended from School	.871***	.133	1.150***	-.044
	(.099)	(.113)	(.236)	(.087)
Arrested	1.217***	.589***	2.716***	.100
	(.125)	(.139)	(.296)	(.094)
Social Class				
Poverty Status	1.038	.180	.334***	
	(.078)	(.113)	(.093)	
Interactions				
Drug Use * Suspended from School	.054	.069	-.056	-.013
	(.035)	(.037)	(.109)	(.062)
Drug Use * Arrested	-.034	.033	-.451***	.021
	(.040)	(.043)	(.105)	(.070)
Drug Use * Poverty Status	.221***	.176***	.157**	-.017
	(.029)	(.033)	(.051)	(.035)

Table A-26. Regressions of dropout on drug use, interactions with social sanctions and poverty status (continued)

	Model 1 Panel Logit No Controls	Model 2 Panel Logit Controls	Model 3 Hybrid Random Effects	
			Between	Within
Suspended from School * Poverty Status	-.528***	-.139	-.906**	-.238
	(.142)	(.161)	(.346)	(.132)
Arrested * Poverty Status	.063	.324	.261	.021
	(.192)	(.222)	(.454)	(.160)
Drug Use * Suspended from School * Poverty Status	-.135*	-.130	-.055	-.056
	(.060)	(.067)	(.184)	(.103)
Drug Use * Arrested * Poverty Status	-.220***	-.247**	-.379	-.153
	(.067)	(.076)	(.202)	(.120)

Note: Estimates are unweighted. Standard errors are in parentheses. Standard errors are corrected for clustering. Model 1 includes no control variables (except dummy variables for survey year, age, region, and birth year, and a continuous variable for exposure time). Model 2 includes all controls. Coefficients are omitted to simplify presentation.

*** $p < .001$ ** $p < .01$ * $p < .05$

Table A-27. Predictors of delinquency, 1997

			Level of Delinquency			
	None	Any	1-2 Offenses	3-4 Offenses	5-6 Offenses	>6 Offenses
Demographics						
Age	15.72	16.04	15.88	16.15	16.26	16.57
Gender						
Male	40.6%	58.5%	53.9%	60.2%	69.0%	74.7%
Female	59.4%	41.5%	46.1%	39.8%	31.0%	25.3%
Race						
White	69.3%	70.0%	68.9%	71.6%	68.7%	73.1%
Black	13.8%	14.4%	16.2%	11.6%	12.0%	12.6%
Hispanic	12.4%	11.4%	10.3%	13.1%	13.5%	11.5%
Asian	2.2%	1.2%	1.2%	1.1%	2.1%	0.0%
Other	2.3%	3.1%	3.3%	2.6%	3.8%	2.8%
Parental Education						
High School	11.0%	12.7%	12.2%	12.6%	14.1%	15.4%
Dropout						
High School	29.9%	30.9%	32.4%	29.2%	25.8%	30.2%
College	59.1%	56.4%	55.4%	58.1%	60.1%	54.4%

Table A-27. Predictors of delinquency, 1997 (continued)

	None	Any	Level of Delinquency 1-2 Offenses	3-4 Offenses	5-6 Offenses	>6 Offenses
1996 Household Income (Log)						
Bottom Quartile	17.9%	19.2%	19.5%	18.5%	20.3%	18.1%
2nd Quartile	27.4%	30.9%	29.8%	32.5%	30.7%	33.6%
3rd Quartile	34.9%	33.0%	33.6%	31.3%	31.4%	35.0%
Top Quartile	37.8%	36.1%	36.6%	36.2%	37.9%	31.4%
Mother < 20 at Birth	11.2%	12.4%	12.2%	11.1%	16.6%	13.9%
Family Structure						
Both Biological Parents	60.4%	49.1%	51.7%	48.8%	44.8%	36.4%
Biological Mother Only	21.3%	26.4%	25.8%	24.4%	28.1%	35.6%
Biological Father Only	2.4%	3.8%	3.1%	5.2%	6.1%	2.0%
Stepparent	12.4%	16.3%	15.3%	17.9%	14.5%	19.8%
Other Parent	3.6%	4.4%	4.0%	3.8%	6.5%	6.2%

Table A-27. Predictors of delinquency, 1997 (continued)

	None	Any	Level of Delinquency 1-2 Offenses	3-4 Offenses	5-6 Offenses	>6 Offenses
Residence						
Rural	33.1%	27.7%	28.2%	25.7%	26.0%	32.4%
Urban	67.4%	72.5%	72.1%	74.3%	74.1%	68.1%
Mother Supportive	2.83	2.70	2.73	2.67	2.69	2.60
Mother Permissive	45.5%	48.3%	45.0%	50.1%	59.4%	54.3%
Residences since Age 12	1.42	1.57	1.49	1.63	1.59	1.87
Schools since 7th Grade	1.35	1.54	1.44	1.63	1.63	1.85
Region						
Northeast	17.3%	16.9%	16.7%	15.9%	15.2%	22.4%
North Central	28.7%	27.6%	28.0%	28.4%	21.9%	27.1%
South	34.2%	34.7%	36.2%	31.6%	41.3%	28.1%
West	19.8%	20.9%	19.1%	24.1%	21.5%	22.4%

Birth Cohort

Table A-27. Predictors of delinquency, 1997 (continued)

			Level of Delinquency			
	None	Any	1-2 Offenses	3-4 Offenses	5-6 Offenses	>6 Offenses
1980	15.2%	20.6%	18.2%	22.3%	22.2%	29.1%
1981	17.7%	20.4%	18.6%	20.5%	26.3%	27.1%
1982	19.0%	21.4%	20.3%	23.3%	20.3%	23.8%
1983	22.4%	18.6%	20.1%	17.5%	17.6%	12.3%
1984	25.6%	19.0%	22.8%	16.4%	13.6%	7.6%
School Performance						
GPA in 8th Grade, 8-Point Scale	4.47	3.91	3.70	3.37	3.60	2.86
Ever Repeated a Grade	11.5%	16.1%	15.1%	14.4%	22.7%	21.7%
School Attachment	8.46	7.69	7.96	7.61	7.14	6.62
Cognitive Ability ASVAB Math-Verbal Score						
Bottom Quintile	12.8%	14.5%	14.7%	11.8%	15.3%	20.8%
2nd Quintile	17.7%	19.7%	18.1%	20.5%	25.3%	23.7%
3rd Quintile	22.6%	25.6%	25.7%	24.8%	20.4%	32.0%

Table A-27. Predictors of delinquency, 1997 (continued)

			Level of Delinquency			
	None	Any	1-2 Offenses	3-4 Offenses	5-6 Offenses	>6 Offenses
4th Quintile	26.4%	28.2%	26.8%	31.0%	32.9%	24.2%
Top Quintile	33.2%	26.5%	29.4%	23.8%	21.4%	20.1%
Peer Environment						
Antisocial Peers	1.91	2.33	2.16	2.43	2.46	3.00
Prosocial Peers	3.16	3.00	3.08	2.93	2.94	2.78
Other Deviant Behavior						
Ever had Sex	11.3%	27.1%	18.8%	28.8%	41.5%	63.4%
Adult Role Transitions						
Ever had a Child	0.7%	0.5%	0.5%	0.3%	0.6%	0.8%
Worked >20 Hours	11.1%	17.3%	14.7%	18.6%	19.6%	27.6%
Ever Married	0.0%	0.0%	0.0%	0.0%	0.0%	0.0%
Living with a Sexual Partner	0.0%	0.2%	0.2%	0.3%	0.0%	0.2%

Note: Data are weighted. Percentages for dummy variables may not add to 100 percent due to rounding and imputation.

Table A-28. Predictors of drug use, 1997

			Level of Drug Use			
	None	Any	1	2	3	>3
Demographics						
Age	15.62	16.54	16.34	16.51	16.82	16.88
Gender						
Male	49.3%	49.7%	46.7%	53.3%	49.3%	54.6%
Female	50.7%	50.3%	53.3%	46.7%	50.7%	45.3%
Race						
White	67.3%	76.0%	74.7%	75.3%	77.4%	80.8%
Black	15.6%	9.9%	11.6%	9.4%	8.9%	6.0%
Hispanic	12.5%	10.4%	9.7%	11.8%	11.2%	9.4%
Asian	2.1%	0.7%	0.9%	0.7%	0.5%	0.0%
Other	2.6%	2.9%	3.1%	2.8%	2.0%	3.9%
Parental Education						
High School Dropout	11.5%	12.7%	13.0%	14.5%	10.5%	10.8%
High School	29.8%	32.0%	33.2%	30.1%	30.1%	33.9%
College	58.7%	55.4%	53.8%	55.5%	59.4%	55.3%

Table A-28. Predictors of drug use, 1997 (continued)

			Level of Drug Use			
	None	Any	1	2	3	>3
1996 Household Income (Log)						
Bottom Quartile	18.4%	18.9%	21.2%	17.8%	16.5%	16.0%
2nd Quartile	28.0%	32.0%	30.7%	31.4%	37.1%	29.9%
3rd Quartile	33.8%	34.2%	41.2%	29.3%	26.2%	31.3%
Top Quartile	38.1%	33.8%	28.1%	39.3%	36.7%	38.8%
Mother < 20 at Birth	11.3%	12.9%	14.0%	11.0%	13.7%	11.6%
Family Structure						
Both Biological Parents	58.0%	46.4%	47.3%	44.9%	45.2%	47.7%
Biological Mother Only	21.8%	29.2%	27.6%	31.4%	29.6%	29.8%
Biological Father Only	2.6%	4.4%	4.1%	5.3%	4.7%	3.1%
Stepparent	13.6%	16.2%	15.8%	16.9%	16.6%	16.0%
Other Parent	4.0%	3.8%	5.2%	1.5%	3.9%	3.3%
Residence						
Rural	30.4%	30.5%	31.8%	29.4%	30.9%	27.4%

Table A-28. Predictors of drug use, 1997 (continued)

	None	Any	Level of Drug Use 1	2	3	>3
Urban	69.8%	69.9%	68.4%	69.9%	70.6%	74.9%
Mother Supportive	2.79	2.71	2.71	2.72	2.70	2.66
Mother Permissive	44.2%	54.0%	50.8%	51.9%	59.8%	62.3%
Region						
Northeast	16.7%	18.3%	19.2%	16.8%	15.5%	22.4%
North Central						
South	34.5%	34.1%	36.8%	32.9%	32.6%	28.3%
West	20.6%	19.5%	16.8%	21.9%	20.3%	24.1%
Birth Cohort						
1980	13.3%	30.0%	25.8%	27.2%	34.5%	41.4%
1981	16.3%	26.4%	23.5%	26.3%	29.5%	31.4%
1982	20.0%	20.7%	20.7%	24.4%	21.1%	14.2%
1983	23.0%	13.9%	17.0%	14.2%	11.3%	7.1%
1984	27.4%	9.0%	13.0%	7.9%	3.6%	5.9%
Residences since Age 12	1.41	1.70	1.71	1.67	1.74	1.62
Schools since 7th Grade	1.3	1.8	1.6	1.7	2.0	1.9

Table A-28. Predictors of drug use, 1997 (continued)

			Level of Drug Use			
	None	Any	1	2	3	>3
School Performance						
GPA in 8th Grade, 8-Point Scale	3.05	3.69	3.57	3.72	3.72	4.09
Ever Repeated a Grade	12.5%	17.2%	16.9%	18.6%	16.0%	16.9%
School Attachment	8.38	7.30	7.54	7.24	7.13	6.78
Cognitive Ability						
ASVAB Math-Verbal Score						
Bottom Quintile	13.3%	14.7%	14.4%	12.2%	13.1%	23.2%
2nd Quintile	17.8%	21.2%	22.6%	20.4%	17.8%	22.6%
3rd Quintile	22.8%	27.4%	26.3%	30.4%	26.2%	26.8%
4th Quintile	26.3%	30.1%	30.1%	29.1%	31.3%	30.4%
Top Quintile	33.1%	21.4%	21.1%	20.1%	24.7%	20.2%
Peer Environment						
Antisocial Peers	1.92	2.64	2.45	2.62	2.84	3.10
Prosocial Peers	3.15	2.90	2.92	2.87	2.91	2.88

Other Deviant Behavior

Table A-28. Predictors of drug use, 1997 (continued)

			Level of Drug Use			
	None	Any	1	2	3	>3
Ever had Sex	10.5%	41.8%	31.3%	43.5%	50.9%	64.9%
Adult Role Transitions						
Ever had a Child	0.4%	1.0%	1.6%	0.5%	0.4%	0.5%
Worked >20 Hours	10.3%	24.2%	21.0%	24.9%	26.9%	31.4%
Ever Married	0.0%	0.0%	0.1%	0.0%	0.0%	0.0%
Living with a Sexual Partner	0.0%	0.3%	0.2%	0.4%	0.6%	0.3%

Note: Data are weighted. Percentages for dummy variables may not add to 100 percent due to rounding and imputation.

References

Agnew, Robert and David M. Petersen. 1989. "Leisure and Delinquency." Social Problems 36:332-350.

Alexander, Karl L., Doris R. Entwisle, and Carrie S. Horsey. 1997. "From First Grade Forward: Early Foundations of High School Dropout." Sociology of Education 70:87-107.

Alexander, Karl L., Doris R. Entwisle, and Nader S. Kabbani. 2001. "The Dropout Process in Life Course Perspective: Early Risk Factors at Home and School." Teachers College Record 103:760-822.

Alliance for Excellent Education. 2003. "Fact Sheet: The Impact of Education On: Health & Well-Being." Washington, DC: Author.

Allison, Paul D. 2002. Missing Data. Thousand Oaks, CA: Sage Publications.

—. 2005. Fixed Effects Regression Methods for Longitudinal Data Using Sas. Cary, NC: SAS Institute.

Archambault, Isabelle, Michel Janosz, Jean-Sabastein Fallu, and Linda Pagani. 2009. "Student Engagement and Its Relationship with Early High School Dropout." Journal of Adolescence 32:651-670.

Astone, Nan Marie and Sara S. McLanahan. 1994. "Family Structure, Residential Mobility, and School Dropout: A Research Note." Demography 31:575-584.

Bachman, Jerald G. 1983. "Premature Affluence: Do High School Students Earn Too Much?" Economic Outlook USA 10:64-67.

—. 2008. The Education-Drug Use Connection : How Successes and Failures in School Relate to Adolescent Smoking, Drinking, Drug Use, and Delinquency. New York: L. Erlbaum Associates.

Bachman, Jerald G., Swayzer Green, and Ilona D. Wirtanen. 1971. Dropping out--Problem or Symptom?, vol. III. Ann Arbor, MI: Institute for Social Research.

Bachman, Jerald G., Patrick M. O'Malley, and Jerome Johnston. 1978. *Adolescence to Adulthood: Change and Stability in the Lives of Young Men*, vol. VI. Ann Arbor, MI: Institute for Social Research.

Bachman, Jerald G. and John Schulenberg. 1993. "How Part-Time Work Intensity Relates to Drug Use, Problem Behavior, Time Use, and Satisfaction among High School Seniors: Are These Consequences or Merely Correlates?" Developmental Psychology 29:220-235.

Barton, Paul E. 2003. "The Closing of the Educational Frontier." Princeton, NJ: Educational Testing Service, Policy Information Center.

—. 2005. "One-Third of a Nation: Rising Dropout Rates and Declining Opportunities." Princeton, NJ: Policy Information Center, Educational Testing Service

Beger, Randall R. 2002. "Expansion of Police Power in Public Schools and the Vanishing Rights of Students." Social Justice 29:119-130.

Bendixen, Mons, Inger M. Endresen, and Dan Olweus. 2003. "Variety and Frequency Scales of Antisocial Involvement: Which One Is Better?" Legal & Criminological Psychology 8:135-150.

Braithwaite, John. 1981. "The Myth of Social Class and Criminality Reconsidered." American Sociological Review 46:36-57.

Bridgeland, John M., John J. DiIulio, Jr., and Karen Burke Morison. 2006. "The Silent Epidemic: Perspectives of High School Dropouts." Washington, DC: Civic Enterprises.

Bryk, Anthony S. and Yeow Meng Thum. 1989. "The Effects of High School Organization on Dropping Out: An Exploratory Investigation." American Educational Research Journal 26:353-383.

Burton, Linda. 2007. "Childhood Adultification in Economically Disadvantaged Families: A Conceptual Model." Family Relations 56:329-345.

Bushway, Shawn, Robert Brame, Raymond Paternoster, and Robert Apel. 2000. "The Relationship between Teenage Employment and Crime in the NLSY97." Washington, DC: U.S Department of Labor.

Cairns, Robert B., Beverley D. Cairns, and Holly J. Neckerman. 1989. "Early School Dropout: Configurations and Determinants." Child Development 60:1437-1452.

Cameron, Stephen V. and James J. Heckman. 1993. "The Nonequivalence of High School Equivalents." Journal of Labor Economics 11:1-47.

Cataldi, Emily Forrest, Jennifer Laird, Angelina KewelRamani, and Chris Chapman. 2009. "High School Dropout and Completion Rates in the United States: 2007." NCES 2009-064. Washington, DC: National Center for Education Statistics.

CHRR. 2003. NLSY97 User's Guide. Washington, DC: U.S. Department of Labor.

—. 2005. NLSY97 User's Guide. Washington, DC: U.S. Department of Labor.

Chuang, Hwei-Lin. 1997. "High School Youths' Dropout and Re-Enrollment Behavior." Economics of Education Review 16:171-186.

Coleman, James Samuel and Thomas Hoffer. 1987. Public and Private High Schools: The Impact of Communities. New York: Basic Books.

Coley, Richard J. 1995. "Dreams Deferred: High School Dropouts in the United States." Princeton, NJ: Educational Testing Service.

Crum, Rosa M., Margaret E. Ensminger, Marguerite J. Ro, and Joan McCord. 1998. "The Association of Educational Attainment and School Dropout with Risk of Alcoholism: A Twenty-Five-Rear Prospective Study of Inner-City Children." Journal of Studies on Alcohol 59:318-326.

Day, Jennifer Cheeseman and Eric C. Newburger. 2002. "The Big Payoff: Educational Attainment and Synthetic Estimates of Work-Life Earnings." Washington, DC: U.S. Census Bureau.

De Li, Spencer. 1999. "Legal Sanctions and Youths' Status Attainment: A Longitudinal Study." JQ: Justice Quarterly 16:377-401.

Dohrn, Bernardine. 2001. "Look out Kid, It's Something You Did: Zero Tolerance for Children." Pp. 89-113 in Zero Tolerance: Resisting the Drive for Punishment in Our Schools, edited by W. Ayers, B. Dohrn, and R. Ayers. New York: New Press.

Doland, E. 2001. "Give Yourself the Gift of a Degree." Employment Policy Foundation.

Donovan, John E. and Richard Jessor. 1985. "Structure of Problem Behavior in Adolescence and Young Adulthood." Journal of Consulting and Clinical Psychology 53:890-904.

Donovan, John E., Richard Jessor, and Frances M. Costa. 1988. "Syndrome of Problem Behavior in Adolescence: A Replication." Journal of Consulting and Clinical Psychology 56:762-765.

Ekstrom, Ruth B., Margaret E. Goertz, Judith M. Pollack, and Donald A. Rock. 1986. "Who Drops out of High School and Why? Findings from a National Study." Teachers College Record 87:356-373.

Ellickson, Phyllis, Khanh Bui, Robert Bell, and Kimberly A. McGuigan. 1998. "Does Early Drug Use Increase the Risk of Dropping out of High School?" Journal of Drug Issues 28:357-380.

Elliott, Delbert S. and David Huizinga. 1983. "Social Class and Delinquent Behavior in a National Youth Panel." Criminology 21:149-177.

Elliott, Delbert S., David Huizinga, and Suzanne S. Ageton. 1985. Explaining Delinquency and Drug Use. Beverly Hills, CA: Sage Publications.

Elliott, Delbert S. and Harwin L. Voss. 1974. Delinquency and Dropout. Lexington, MA: Lexington Books.

Ensminger, Margaret E. and Anita L. Slusarcick. 1992. "Paths to High School Graduation or Dropout: A Longitudinal Study of a First-Grade Cohort." Sociology of Education 65:95-113.

Entwisle, Doris R., Karl L. Alexander, and Linda Steffel Olson. 2004. "Temporary as Compared to Permanent High School Dropout." Social Forces 82:1181-1205.

Evans, William N. and Robert M. Schwab. 1995. "Finishing High School and Starting College: Do Catholic Schools Make a Difference?" The Quarterly Journal of Economics 110:941-974.

Fagan, Jeffrey and Edward Pabon. 1990. "Contributions of Delinquency and Substance Use to School Dropout among Inner-City Youths." Youth & Society 21:306-354.

Farnworth, Margaret, Lawrence J. Schweinhart, and John R. Berrueta-Clement. 1985. "Preschool Intervention, School Success and Delinquency in a High-Risk Sample of Youth." American Educational Research Journal 22:445-464.

Fernandez, Roberto M., Ronnelle Paulsen, and Marsha Hirano-Nakanishi. 1989. "Dropping out among Hispanic Youth." Social Science Research 18:21-52.

Finn, Jeremy D. 1989. "Withdrawing from School." Review of Educational Research 59:117-142.

—. 1991. "How to Make the Dropout Problem Go Away." Educational Researcher 20:28-30.

Flisher, Alan J., Loraine Townsend, Perpetual Chikobvu, Carl F. Lombard, and Gary King. 2010. "Ubstance Use and Psychosocial Predictors of High School Dropout in Cape Town, South Africa." Journal of Research on Adolescence 20:237-255.

Friedman, Alfred S., Nita Glickmand, and Arlene Utada. 1983. "Does Drug and Alcohol Use Lead to Failure to Graduate from High School?" Journal of Drug Education 15:353-365.

Frisco, Michelle L. 2008. "Adolescents' Sexual Behavior and Academic Attainment." Sociology of Education 81:284-311.

Gasper, Joseph, Stefanie DeLuca, and Angela Estacion. 2010. "Coming and Going: Explaining the Effects of Residential and School Mobility on Adolescent Delinquency." Social Science Research 39:459-476.

Goldschmidt, Pete and Jia Wang. 1999. "When Can Schools Affect Dropout Behavior? A Longitudinal Multilevel Analysis." American Educational Research Journal 36:715-738.

Gottfredson, Gary D. and Denise C. Gottfredson. 1985. Victimization in Schools. New York: Plenum Press.

Gove, Walter R. and Robert D. Crutchfield. 1982. "The Family and Juvenile Delinquency*." The Sociological Quarterly 23:301-319.

Greene, Jay P. and Marcus A. Winters. 2006. "Leaving Boys Behind: Public High School Graduation Rates " New York: Center for Civic Innovation, Manhatten Institute.

Greene, William H. 2003. Econometric Analysis. Upper Saddle River, NJ: Prentice Hall.

Hagan, John. 1997. "Defiance and Despair: Subcultural and Structural Linkages between Delinquency and Despair in the Life Course." Social Forces 76:119-134.

Hannon, Lance. 2003. "Poverty, Delinquency, and Educational Attainment: Cumulative Disadvantage or Disadvantage Saturation?" Sociological Inquiry 73:575-594.

Harlow, Caroline Wolf. 2003. "Education and Correctional Populations." Washington, DC: U.S. Department of Justice.

Hathaway, Starke R., Phyllis C. Reynolds, and Elio D. Monachesi. 1969. "Follow-up of the Later Careers and Lives of 1,000 Boys Who Dropped out of High School." Journal of Consulting and Clinical Psychology 33:370-380.

Hauser, Robert M., Solon J. Simmons, and Devah I. Pager. 2004. "High School Dropout: Race/Ethnicity, and Social Background from the 1970s to the 1990s." Pp. 85-106 in Dropouts in America: Confronting the Graduation Rate Crisis, edited by G. Orfield. Cambridge, MA: Harvard Education Press.

Heckman, James J. and V. Joseph Hotz. 1989. "Choosing among Alternative Nonemperimental Methods for Estimating the Impact of Social Programs: The Case of Manpower Training: Rejoinder." Journal of the American Statistical Association 84:878-880.

Heckman, James J., Lance J. Lochner, and Petra E. Todd. 2008. "Earnings Functions and Rates of Return." Journal of Human Capital 2:1-31.

Hindelang, Michael J., Travis Hirschi, and Joseph G. Weis. 1981. Measuring Delinquency. Beverly Hills, CA: Sage Publications.

Hirschfield, Paul. 2009. "Another Way Out: The Impact of Juvenile Arrests on High School Dropout." Sociology of Education 82:368-393.

Hsiao, Cheng. 2003. Analysis of Panel Data. Cambridge, MA: Cambridge University Press.

Jackson, Toby. 1983. "Violence in School." Pp. 1-47 in Crime and Justice: An Annual Review of Research, edited by M. Tonry and N. Morris. Chicago: University of Chicago Press.

Janosz, Michel, Isabelle Archambault, Julien Morizot, and Linda S. Pagani. 2008. "School Engagement Trajectories and Their Differential Predictive Relations to Dropout." Journal of Social Issues 64:21-40.

Janosz, Michel and Marc Le Blanc. 1997. "Deviant Behavior and School Dropout: An Examination of Family, School, and Peer Mediating Processes." Presented at annual meeting of the American Society of Criminology, November 19, 1997, San Diego, CA.

Janosz, Michel, Marc Le Blanc, and Bernard Boulerice. 1998. "Consommation De Psychotropes Et Délinquance: De Bons Prédicteurs De L'abandon Scolaire?" Criminologie XXXI:87-107.

Jarjoura, G. Roger. 1996. "The Conditional Effect of Social Class on the Dropout-Delinquency Relationship." Journal of Research in Crime and Delinquency 33:232-255.

Jessor, Richard, John Edward Donovan, and Frances Marie Costa. 1991. Beyond Adolescence: Problem Behavior and Young Adult Development. New York: Cambridge University Press.

Jessor, Richard and Shirley L. Jessor. 1977. Problem Behavior and Psychosocial Development: A Longitudinal Study of Youth. New York: Academic Press.

Jimerson, Shane R. , Gabrielle E. Anderson, and Angela D. Whipple. 2002. "Winning the Battle and Losing the War: Examining the Relation between Grade Retention and Dropping out of High School." Psychology in the Schools 39:441-457.

Johnston, L. D., P. M. O'Malley, J. G. Bachman, and J. E. Schulenberg. 2008. "Various Stimulant Drugs Show Continuing Gradual Declines among Teens in 2008, Most Illicit Drugs Hold Steady." University of Michigan News Service Retrieved 02/09/2009 (http://www.monitoringthefuture.org).

Kandel, Denise B. 1989. "Issues of Sequencing of Adolescent Drug Use and Other Problem Behaviors." Journal of Drug Issues 53:55-76.

Kaplan, Howard B. and Xiaoru Liu. 1994. "A Longitudinal Analysis of Mediating Variables in the Drug Use-Dropping out Relationship." Criminology 32:415-439.

Kim, Julia Yun Soo, Michael Fendrich, and Joseph S. Wislar. 2000. "The Validity of Juvenile Arrestees' Drug Use Reporting: A Gender Comparison." Journal of Research in Crime and Delinquency 37:419-432.

Krohn, Marvin D., Alan J. Lizotte, and Cynthia M. Perez. 1997. "The Interrelationship between Substance Use and Precocious Transitions to Adult Statuses." Journal of Health and Social Behavior 38:87-103.

Krohn, Marvin D., Terence P. Thornberry, Lori Collins-Hall, and Alan J. Lizotte. 1995. "School Dropout, Delinquent Behavior, and Drug Use: An Examination of the Causes and Consequences of Dropping out of School." Pp. 163-183 in Drugs, Crime, and Other Deviant Adaptations: Longitudinal Studies, edited by H. B. Kaplan. New York: Plenum Press.

Liska, Allen E. and Mark D. Reed. 1985. "Ties to Conventional Institutions and Delinquency: Estimating Reciprocal Effects." American Sociological Review 50:547-560.

Maguin, Eugene and Rolf Loeber. 1996. "Academic Performance and Delinquency." Crime and Justice 20:145-264.

Mann, Dale. 1987. "Can We Help Dropouts? Thinking About the Undoable." Pp. 3-20 in School Dropouts: Patterns and Policies, edited by G. Natriello. New York: Teachers College Press.

Marsh, Herbert W. 1991. "Employment During High School: Character Building or a Subversion of Academic Goals?" Sociology of Education 64:172-189.

Maxfield, Michael G., Barbara Luntz Weiler, and Cathy Spatz Widom. 2000. "Comparing Self-Reports and Official Records of Arrests." Journal of Quantitative Criminology 16:87-110.

Mayer, Susan. 1991. "How Much Does a High School's Racial and Socioeconomic Mix Affect Graduation and Teenage Fertility Rates?" Pp. 321-341 in The Urban Underclass, edited by C. Jencks and P. Peterson. Washington, DC: Brookings Institution.

McCaffery, Daniel F., Rosalie Liccardo Pacula, Bing Han, and Phyllis Ellickson. 2010. "Marijuana Use and High School Dropout: The Influence of Unobservables." Health Economics 19:1281-1299.

McCluskey, Cynthia Perez, Marvin D. Krohn, Alan J. Lizotte, and Monica L. Rodriguez. 2002. "Early Substance Use and School Achievement: An Examination of Latino, White, and African American Youth." Journal of Drug Issues 32:921-943.

McNeal, Ralph B. 1997. "High School Dropouts: A Closer Examination of School Effects." Social Science Quarterly (University of Texas Press) 78:209-222.

Mensch, Barbara and Denise B. Kandel. 1992. "Drug Use as a Risk Factor for Premarital Teen Pregnancy and Abortion in a National Sample of Young White Women." Demography 29:409-429.

Mensch, Barbara S. and Denise B. Kandel. 1988. "Dropping Out of High School and Drug Involvement." Sociology of Education 61:95-113.

Miao, Jing and Walt Haney. 2004. "High School Graduation Rates: Alternative Methods and Implications." Education Policy Analysis Archives 12. Retrieved August 29, 2006 (http://epaa.asu.edu/epaa/v12n55).

Michael, Robert T. and Michael R. Pergamit. 2001. "The National Longitudinal Survey of Youth, 1997 Cohort." The Journal of Human Resources 36:628-640.

Moffitt, Terrie E. 1993. "Adolescence-Limited and Life-Course-Persistent Antisocial Behavior: A Developmental Taxonomy." Psychological Review 100:674-701.

Mott, Frank L. and R. Jean Haurin. 1988. "Linkages between Sexual Activity and Alcohol and Drug Use among American Adolescents." Family Planning Perspectives 20:128-136.

Mott, Frank L. and William Marsiglio. 1985. "Early Childbearing and Completion of High School." Family Planning Perspectives 17:234-237.

Neal, Derek. 1997. "The Effects of Catholic Secondary Schooling on Educational Achievement." Journal of Labor Economics 15:98-123.

Newcomb, Michael D. and Peter M. Bentler. 1988. Consequences of Adolescent Drug Use: Impact on the Lives of Young Adults. Newbury Park, CA: Sage Publications.

Obot, Isidore Silas and James C. Anthony. 2000. "School Dropout and Injecting Drug Use in a National Sample of White Non-Hispanic American Adults." Journal of Drug Education 30:145-155.

Olson, Randall J. 2005. "The Problem of Respondent Attrition: Survey Methodology Is Key." Monthly Labor Review 128:63-70.

Osgood, D. Wayne, Lloyd D. Johnston, Patrick M. O'Malley, and Jerald G. Bachman. 1988. "The Generality of Deviance in Late Adolescence and Early Adulthood." American Sociological Review 53:81-93.

Osgood, D. Wayne, Barbara J. McMorris, and Maria T. Potenza. 2002. "Analyzing Multiple-Item Measures of Crime and Deviance I: Item Response Theory Scaling." Journal of Quantitative Criminology 18:267-296.

Parker, Jeffrey G. and Steven R. Asher. 1987. "Peer Relations and Later Personal Adjustment: Are Low-Accepted Children at Risk?" Psychological Bulletin 102:357-389.

Paschall, Mallie J., Miriam L. Ornstein, and Robert L. Flewelling. 2001. "African American Male Adolescents' Involvement in the Criminal Justice System: The Criterion Validity of Self-Report Measures in a Prospective Study." Journal of Research in Crime and Delinquency 38:174-187.

Paternoster, Raymond, Shawn Bushway, Robert Brame, and Robert Apel. 2003. "The Effect of Teenage Employment on Delinquency and Problem Behaviors." Social Forces 82:297-335.

Pierret, Charles, Alison Aughinbaugh, A. Rupa Datta, and Tricia
    Gladden. 2007. "Event History Data: Lessons from the NLSY97."
    Presented at Conference on the Event History Calendar Method,
    Organized by the University of Michigan's Panel Study on Income
    Dynamics (PSID) and the U.S. Census Bureau, December 5-6,
    Washington, DC.

Piquero, Alex R., Randall Macintosh, and Matthew Hickman. 2002.
    "The Validity of a Self-Reported Delinquency Scale: Comparisons
    across Gender, Age, Race, and Place of Residence." Sociological
    Methods Research 30:492-529.

Pirog, Maureen A. and Chris Magee. 1997. "High School Completion:
    The Influence of Schools, Families, and Adolescent Parenting."
    Social Science Quarterly (University of Texas Press) 78:710-724.

Plank, Stephen B., Stefanie DeLuca, and Angela Estacion. 2008. "High
    School Dropout and the Role of Career and Technical Education:
    A Survival Analysis of Surviving High School." Sociology of
    Education 81:345-370.

Rebellon, Cesar J. 2002. "Reconsidering the Broken
    Homes/Delinquency Relationship and Exploring Its Mediating
    Mechanism(S)*." Criminology 40:103-136.

Riehl, Carolyn. 1999. "Labeling and Letting Go: An Organizational
    Analysis of How High School Students Are Discharged as
    Dropouts." Pp. 231-268 in Research in Sociology of Education,
    edited by A. M. Pallas. New York: JAI Press.

Rouse, Cecilia E. 2005. "The Labor Market Consequences of an
    Inadequate Education." Presented at symposium on the social costs
    of inadequate education, October 2005, Teachers College.

Rumberger, Russell W. 1983. "Dropping out of High School: The
    Influence of Race, Sex, and Family Background." American
    Educational Research Journal 20:199-220.

—. 1987. "High School Dropouts: A Review of Issues and Evidence."
    Review of Educational Research 57:101-121.

—. 1995. "Dropping out of Middle School: A Multilevel Analysis of
    Students and Schools." American Educational Research Journal
    32:583-625.

—. 2004. "Why Students Drop Out of School." Pp. 131-156 in
    Dropouts in America: Confronting the Graduation Rate Crisis,
    edited by G. Orfield. Cambridge, MA: Harvard Education Press.

Rumberger, Russell W. and Katherine A. Larson. 1998. "Student Mobility and the Increased Risk of High School Dropout." American Journal of Education 107:1-35.

Rumberger, Russell W. and Scott L. Thomas. 2000. "The Distribution of Dropout and Turnover Rates among Urban and Suburban High Schools." Sociology of Education 73:39-67.

Sampson, Robert J. 1986. "Effects of Socioeconomic Context on Official Reaction to Juvenile Delinquency." American Sociological Review 51:876-885.

Sampson, Robert J. and John H. Laub. 1993. Crime in the Making: Pathways and Turning Points through Life. Cambridge, MA: Harvard University Press.

—. 1997. "A Life-Course Theory of Cumulative Disadvantage and the Stability of Delinquency." Pp. 133-161 in Developmental Theories of Crime and Delinquency, vol. 7, edited by T. P. Thornberry. New Brunswick, NJ: Transaction Press.

Sander, William and Anthony C. Krautmann. 1995. "Catholic Schools, Dropout Rates and Educational Attainment." Economic Inquiry 33:217-233.

Schneider, Barbara L. and David Stevenson. 1999. The Ambitious Generation: America's Teenagers, Motivated but Directionless. New Haven, CT: Yale University Press.

Schwartz, Wendy. 1995. "School Dropouts: New Information About an Old Problem." New York: ERIC Clearinghouse on Urban Education.

Sealock, Miriam D. and Sally S. Simpson. 1998. "Unraveling Bias in Arrest Decisions: The Role of Juvenile Offender Type-Scripts." Justice Quarterly 15:427-457.

Shanahan, Michael J. and Brian P. Flaherty. 2001. "Dynamic Patterns of Time Use in Adolescence." Child Development 72:385-401.

Skiba, Russell J., Reece L. Peterson, and Tara Williams. 1997. "Office Referrals and Suspension: Disciplinary Intervention in Middle Schools." Education & Treatment of Children 20:295-315.

Snyder, Howard N. 2008. "Juvenile Arrests 2005." Washington, DC: Office of Juvenile Justice and Delinquency Prevention.

Staff, Jeremy and Derek Kreager. 2007. "Too Cool for School? Peer Status and High School Dropout." Presented at the annual meeting of the American Sociological Association, August 11, New York, NY.

Staff, Jeremy and Jennifer C. Lee. 2007. "When Work Matters: The Varying Impact of Work Intensity on High School Dropout." Sociology of Education 80:158-178.

Steinberg, Laurence and Shelli Avenevoli. 1998. "Disengagement from School and Problem Behavior in Adolescence: A Developmental-Contextual Analysis of the Influences of Family and Part-Time Work." Pp. 392-424 in New Perspectives on Adolescent Risk Behavior, edited by R. Jessor. New York: Cambridge University Press.

Steinberg, Laurence, B. Brown, and Sanford Dornbusch. 1996. Beyond the Classroom. New York: Simon and Schuster.

Stillwell, Robert. 2010. "Public School Graduates and Dropouts from the Common Core of Data: School Year 2007-08 (Nces 2010-341)." Washington, DC: National Center of Education Statistics, Institute for Education Sciences, U.S. Department of Education.

Streeter, Calvin L. and Cynthia Franklin. 1991. "Psychological and Family Differences between Middle Class and Low Income Dropouts: A Discriminant Analysis." The High School Journal 74:211-219.

Sum, Andrew, Ishwar Khatiwada, Nathan Pond, Mykhaylo Trub'skyy, Neeta Fogg, and Sheila Palma. 2003. "Left Behind in the Labor Market: Labor Market Problems of the Nation's out-of-School, Young Adult Populations." Boston, MA: Center for Labor Market Studies, Northeastern University.

Swanson, Christopher B. and Duncan Chaplin. 2003. "Counting High School Graduates When Graduates Count: Measuring Graduation Rates under the High Stakes of NCLB." Washington, DC: The Urban Institute.

Swanson, Christopher B. and Barbara Schneider. 1999. "Students on the Move: Residential and Educational Mobility in America's Schools." Sociology of Education 72:54-67.

Sweeten, Gary. 2006. "Who Will Graduate? Disruption of High School Education by Arrest and Court Involvement." JQ: Justice Quarterly 23:462-480.

Tanner, Julian, Scott Davies, and Bill O'Grady. 1999. "Whatever Happened to Yesterday's Rebels? Longitudinal Effects of Youth Delinquency on Education and Employment." Social Problems 46:250-274.

Teachman, Jay D., Kathleen Paasch, and Karen Carver. 1996. "Social Capital and Dropping Out of School Early." Journal of Marriage and the Family 58:773-783.

Thornberry, Terence P. and Marvin D. Krohn. 2000. "The Self-Reported Method for Measuring Delinquency and Crime." Criminal Justice 4:33-83.

—. 2001. "The Development of Delinquency: An Interactional Perspective." Pp. 289-305 in Handbook of Youth and Justice, edited by H. R. White.

Thornberry, Terence P., Melanie Moore, and R. L. Christenson. 1985. "The Effect of Dropping out of High School on Subsequent Criminal Behavior." Criminology 23:3-18.

Thornburgh, Nathan 2006. "Dropout Nation." Time, April.

Tittle, Charles R., Wayne J. Villemez, and Douglas A. Smith. 1978. "The Myth of Social Class and Criminality: An Empirical Assessment of the Empirical Evidence." American Sociological Review 43:643-656.

Tracy, Paul E. Jr. 1990. "Prevalence, Incidence, Rates, and Other Descriptive Measurements." Pp. 51-77 in Measurement Issues in Criminology, edited by K. Kempf. New York: Springer-Verlag.

Tremblay, R. E., B. Masse, D. Perron, and M. Leblanc. 1992. "Early Disruptive Behavior, Poor School Achievement, Delinquent Behavior, and Delinquent Personality: Longitudinal Analyses." Journal of Consulting and Clinical Psychology 60:64-72.

Wang, Yongyi and Parvati Krishnamurty. 2008. "Interview Model Effects in the NLSY97 Round 4 and Round 5." Presented at the annual meeting of the American Association for Public Opinion Research, June 28, 2008, Phoenix, AZ.

Warren, John Robert. 2002. "Reconsidering the Relationship between Student Employment and Academic Outcomes: A New Theory and Better Data." Youth & Society 33:366-393.

Warren, John Robert and Andrew Halpern-Manners. 2007. "Is the Glass Empty or Filling Up? Reconciling Divergent Trends in High School Completion and Dropout." Educational Researcher 36:335-343.

Warren, John Robert and Jennifer C. Lee. 2003. "The Impact of Adolescent Employment on High School Dropout: Differences by Individual and Labor-Market Characteristics." Social Science Research 32:98-128.

Wehlage, Gary G. and Robert A. Rutter. 1986. "Dropping Out: How Much Do Schools Contribute to the Problem?" Teachers College Record 87:374-392.

White, Helen Raskin, Marsha E. Bates, and Erich Labouvie. 1998. "Adult Outcomes of Adolescent Drug Use: A Comparison of Process-Oriented and Incremental Analyses." Pp. 150-181 in New Perspectives of Adolescent Risk Behavior, edited by R. Jessor. New York: Cambridge University Press.

Wu, Shi-Chang, William Pink, Robert Crain, and Oliver Moles. 1982. "Student Suspension: A Critical Reappraisal." The Urban Review 14:245-303.

Zagorsky, Jay L. and Rosella Gardecki. 1998. "What Have Researchers Learned from the National Longitudinal Surveys?" Journal of Economic & Social Measurement 25:35-57.

Index

"at risk" youth, 4

abstainers, 89

accelerated role transitions.
See adult role transitions

achievement, 20, 95

adolescence, 1, 2, 15, 19, 26,
85, 89, 90, 92, 94, 95, 96,
98

adult role transitions, 14, 18,
60, 84, 93,

adulthood, 1, 2, 16, 31, 85, 86,
87, 91, 92

adultification, 90

age-inappropriate behavior, 3,
19, 25

alcohol, 2, 9, 11, 17, 18, 37,
68, 69, 72, 85, 86, 88, 89,
98

Alexander, Karl L., 9, 10, 93,
94, 98

Allison, Paul D., 45, 47

arrest, ix, 6, 23, 39, 45, 50, 51,
52, 76, 77, 79, 80, 91, 92,
99

Astone, Nan, 10

attachment to school, 21, 42,
60, 86

audio computer-assisted self-
interview, 34

Bachman, Jerald, 2, 9, 11, 15,
18, 27, 85

Bentler, Peter M., 3, 12, 13,
16, 83, 85, 88

Catholic schools, 10

Chaplin, Duncan, 1, 8

childbearing. *See* teenage
pregnancy

childhood, 92, 95, 98

Christenson, R. L., 11

cigarettes, 37, 59, 67, 68, 86,
88, 89, 98

Coleman, James, 10

commitment to school, 3, 14

Common Core of Data, 7

compulsory school attendance,
97

Crum, Rosa M., 9

cumulative disadvantage
theory, 21

Current Population Survey, 7

DeLuca, Stefanie, 50, 60

deviance proneness, 16

diploma, 1, 7, 8, 9, 32, 81, 87,
91, 9

disadvantage saturation, 22,
23, 92

disciplinary policies, 98

disengagement, 2, 3, 6, 9, 10,
13, 25, 46, 94, 95, 98

dropout prevention, 5, 97, 98
dropping out
    causes of, 9
    consequences of, 8
drug use "lifestyle", 85
educational attainment, 7, 8,
    22, 92
Ekstrom, Ruth B., 9, 10, 11,
    20, 23
Ellickson, Phyllis, 13
Elliott, Del, 2, 10, 11, 35
employment, 18, 21, 42, 87,
    88, 93, 95
Ensminger, Margaret E., 10,
    94
Entwisle, Doris R., 9, 10, 98
Estacion, Angela, 50
Fagan, Jeffrey, 3, 13, 27, 62
family processes, 26, 96
Finn, Jeremy D., 12, 13, 33, 95
fixed effects models, 28, 47,
    59
Franklin, Cynthia, 4, 20, 21,
    22, 24
frequency scale, 35, 36, 69, 71
frustration-self-esteem model,
    12
Gasper, Joseph M., 50
GED, 7, 8, 32, 98, 104
grade retention, 41, 61, 84, 86,
    93
Green, Swayzer, 9
Greene, Jay P., 1, 8, 47
Hannon, Lance, 22, 92
Hoffer, Thomas, 10
Horsey, Karen, 10
Hsiao, Cheng, 47
inability to delay gratification,
    16, 25, 87
Janosz, Michel, 3, 9, 18, 19,
    20, 25, 28

Jessor, Richard, 3, 15, 17, 21,
    83
Johnston, Jerome, 2
Kandel, Denise, 2, 3, 11, 13,
    14, 28, 32, 89, 93, 98
Kaplan, Howard B., 3, 18, 33,
    65
Krohn, Marvin D., 2, 3, 13, 14,
    18, 27, 38, 62, 66, 97
Laub, John H., 21, 26
life course perspective, 10, 94
Liu, Xiaoru, 3, 18, 33, 65
living independently, 2
Lower-class dropouts, 4, 20
maladjusted dropouts, 19, 25
marijuana, 17, 36, 37, 58, 59,
    67, 68, 88, 89
maturity gap, 85, 89, 90
McCaffery, Daniel F., 3, 15
McLanahan, Sarah, 10
Mensch, Barbara, 2, 3, 11, 13,
    14, 28, 32, 93, 98
middle school, 10, 41, 57, 60
middle-class dropouts, 6, 20,
    22, 24, 28, 90
Moore, Melanie, 11
multiple imputation, 45
Newcomb, Michael D., 3, 12,
    13, 16, 83, 85, 87, 88
nonconventionality, 15, 83
occupational attainment, 2
O'Malley, Patrick M., 2
Pabon, Edward, 3, 13, 14, 27,
    62
parents, 2, 3, 12, 18, 21, 22,
    26, 34, 37, 41, 44, 56, 60,
    62, 85, 86, 87, 89, 95, 96
participation-identification
    model, 13
peers, 9, 14, 16, 57, 60, 87, 89,
    93
Plank, Stephen, 60

poverty, 21, 22, 39, 43, 45, 50,
    51, 54, 56, 57, 73, 74, 75,
    76, 77, 79
precocious development
    theory, 15, 16, 18, 85
premature affluence, 85
private schools, 8, 10
problem behavior theory, 15,
    17, 83, 85
psuedomaturity, 16
psychosocial adjustment, 4, 25
puberty, 89
public schools, 10
quiet dropouts, 19
random assignment, 26
random effects models, 28, 43,
    47, 62, 64, 79, 82
returning dropouts, 33
Rumberger, Russell W., 1, 7,
    9, 10, 20, 42, 93
Sampson, Robert J., 21, 23, 26
Schneider, Barbara, 9, 42, 93,
    193, 194
school mobility, 9, 93
school performance, 9, 12, 13,
    41, 67, 83, 84, 89, 94, 95,
    96
school processes, 10
School resources, 10
school resources officers, 99
School structure, 10
selection on observables, 26

self-esteem, 12, 13, 95
self-image, 24, 92, 96
Sexual intercourse, 84, 93
social capital, 21
socioeconomic status, 10, 13,
    41, 50, 60, 94
status dropout rate, 7
Streeter, Calvin L., 4, 20, 21,
    22, 24
student-teacher ratios, 10
suburban schools, 10
suspension, 6, 21, 23, 39, 45,
    51, 52, 76, 77, 80
Swanson, Christopher B., 1, 8,
    9, 42, 93
syndrome, 15, 16, 18, 19, 24,
    83, 84, 87, 89, 95
teachers, 13, 42, 86, 92, 96
teenage pregnancy, 2, 18
Thornberry, Terrence P., 11,
    38, 97
transition proneness, 85
underreporting of delinquency
    by minority youth, 39
urban schools, 10
variety scale, 36, 37, 64, 69,
    70, 71, 74
Voss, Harwin, 2, 10, 11
Warren, John Robert, 8, 9, 93
Wirtanen, Ilona D., 9
zero tolerance, 98

Criminal Justice
Recent Scholarship

Edited by
Marilyn McShane and Frank P. Williams III

A Series from LFB Scholarly